RECORDED VERSIONS
GUITAR

AUTHENTIC TRANSCRIPTIONS
WITH NOTES AND TABLATURE

DON'T YOU FAKE IT

T0039519

Music transcriptions by Addi Booth and Pete Billmann

ISBN-13: 978-1-4234-2749-0
ISBN-10: 1-4234-2749-1

HAL•LEONARD®
CORPORATION

7777 W. BLUEMOUND RD. P.O. BOX 13819 MILWAUKEE, WI 53213

Visit Hal Leonard Online at
www.halleonard.com

In Fate's Hands

Words and Music by Ronnie Winter

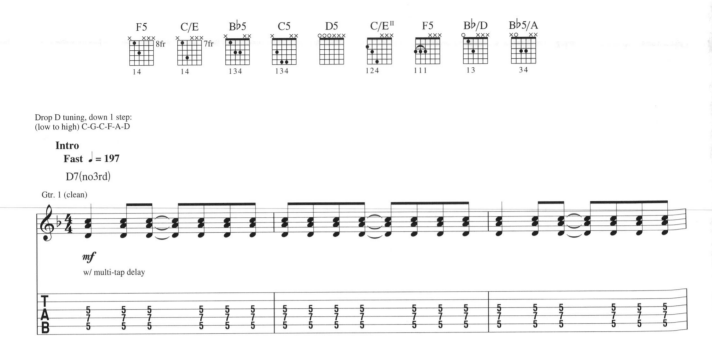

Drop D tuning, down 1 step:
(low to high) C-G-C-F-A-D

Intro
Fast ♩ = 197

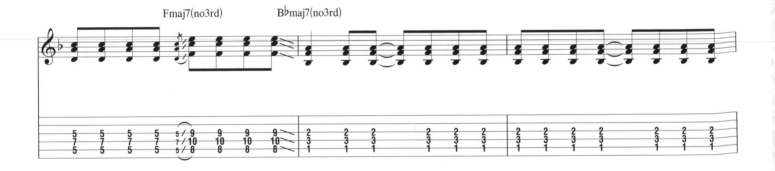

*Doubled throughout

**Chord symbols reflect implied harmony.

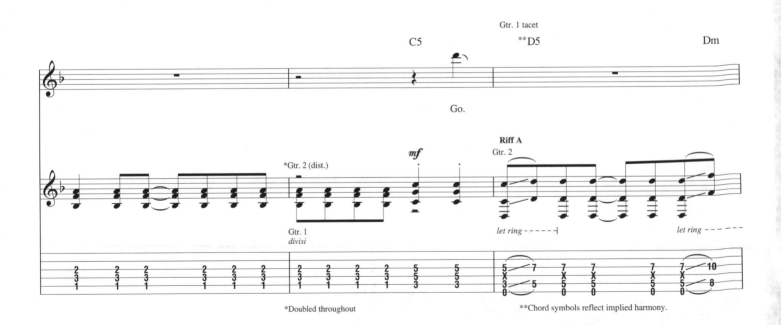

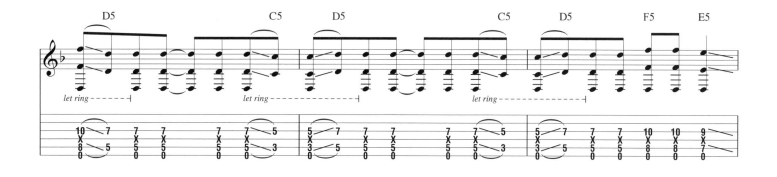

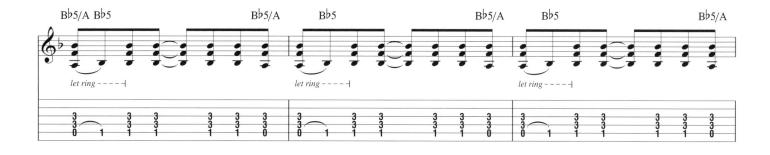

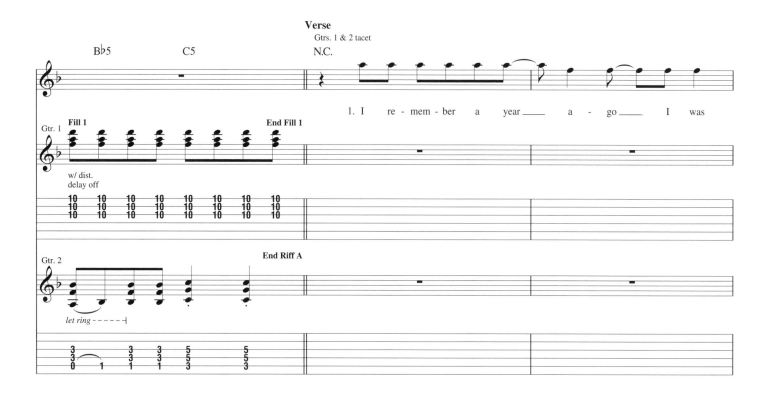

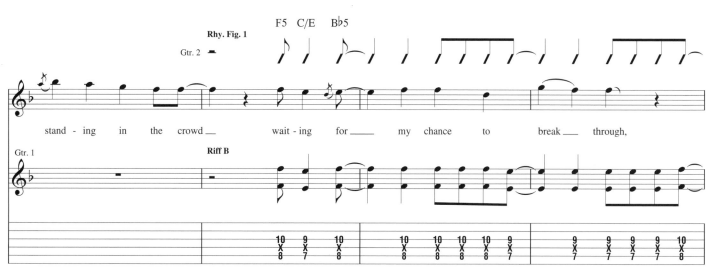

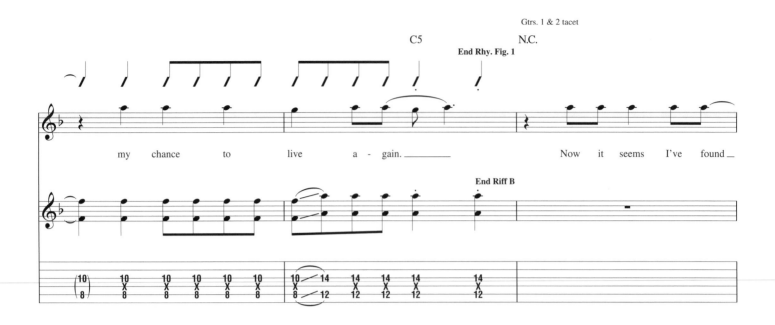

my chance to live a - gain. _____ Now it seems I've found _

_ some friends _ who fi - nal - ly un - der - stand _____ what it takes _

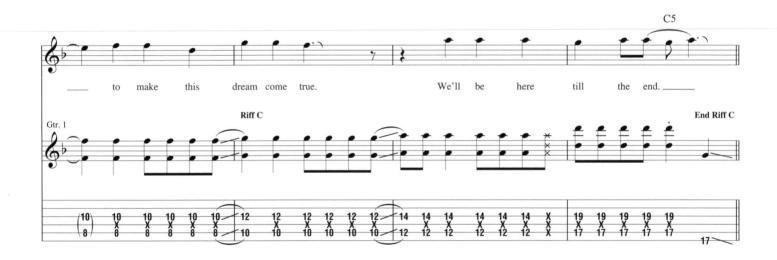

_ to make this dream come true. We'll be here till the end. _____

𝄋 Chorus

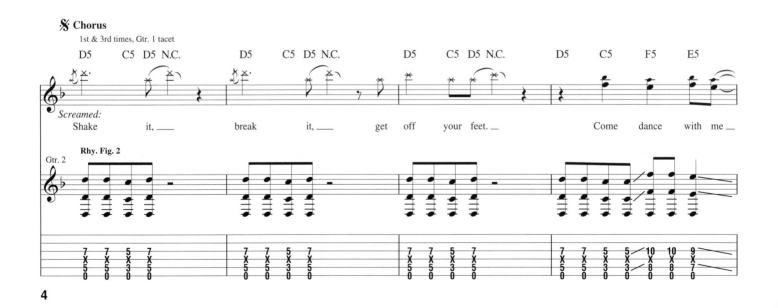

Screamed:

Shake it, _____ break it, _____ get off your feet. _ Come dance with me _

Interlude

Gtr. 1 tacet

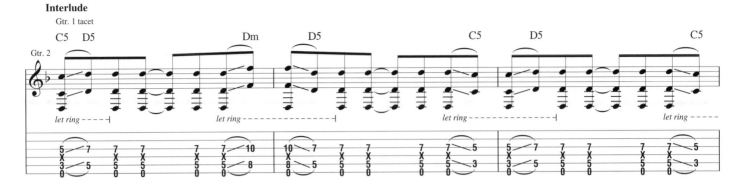

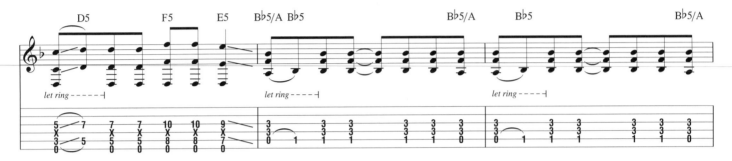

Verse

*Refers to upstemmed voc. only.

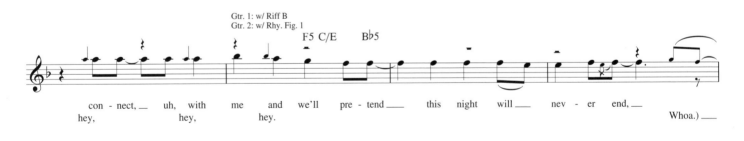

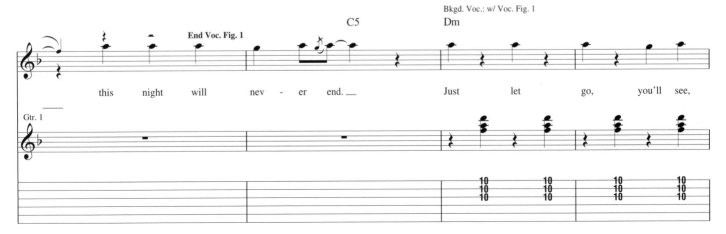

D.S. al Coda 1

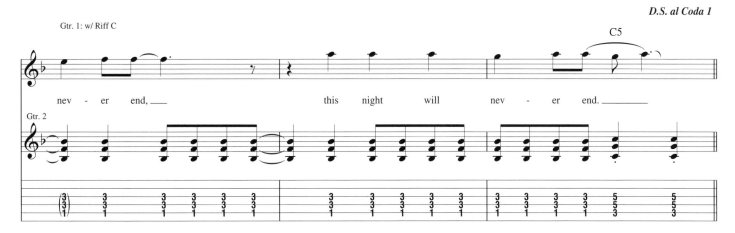

Coda 1
Bridge
Half-time feel

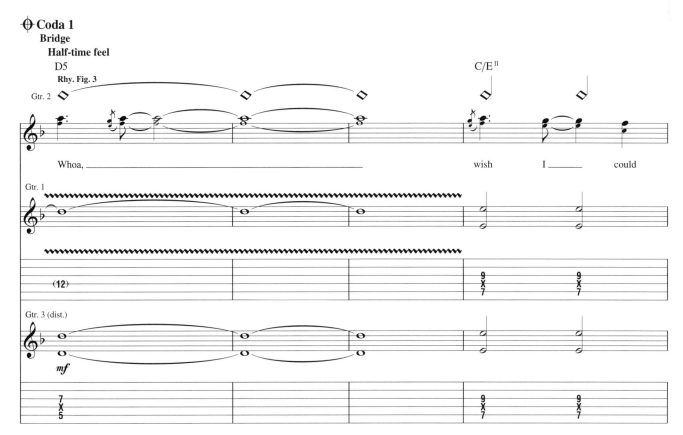

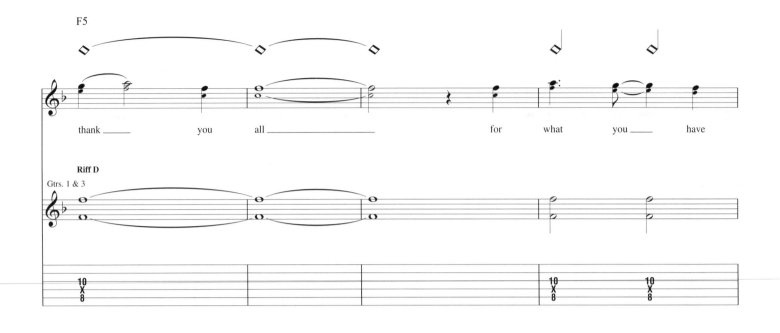

thank ____ you all ____ for what you ____ have

Riff D

Gtrs. 1 & 3

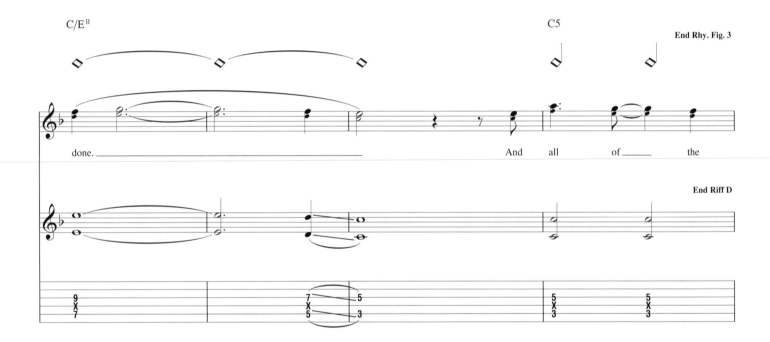

done. _____ And all of ____ the

End Rhy. Fig. 3

End Riff D

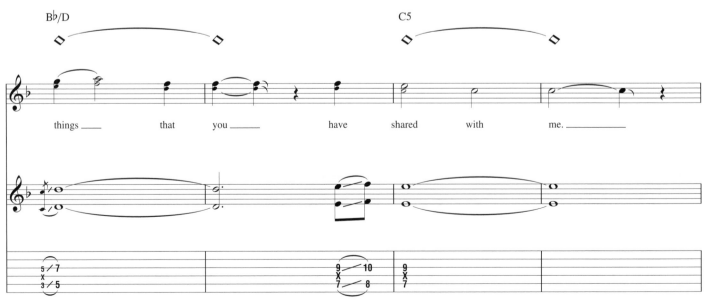

things ____ that you ____ have shared with me. ____

Gtr. 2: w/ Rhy. Fig. 3

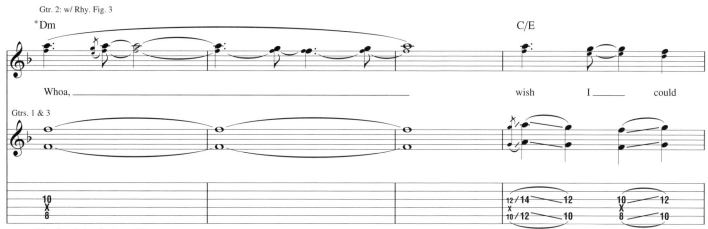

*Chord symbols reflect overall harmony.

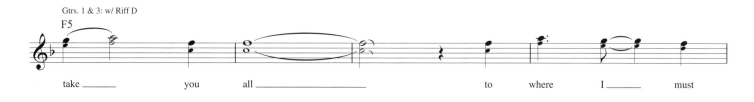

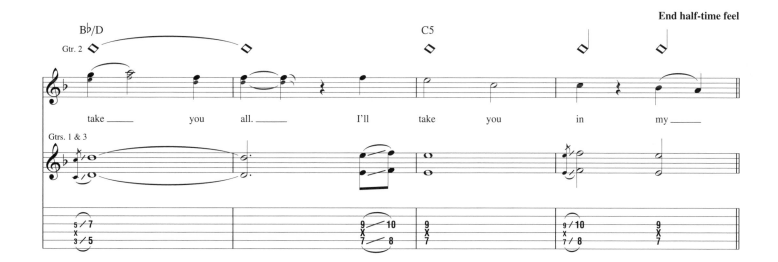

Interlude

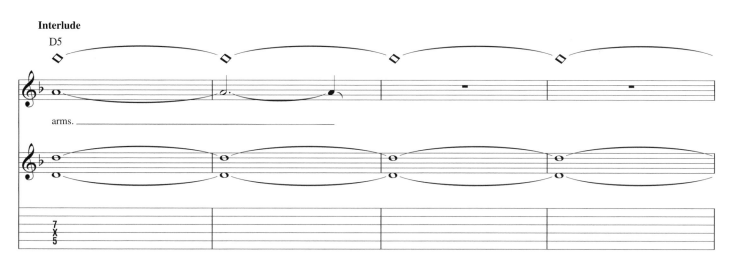

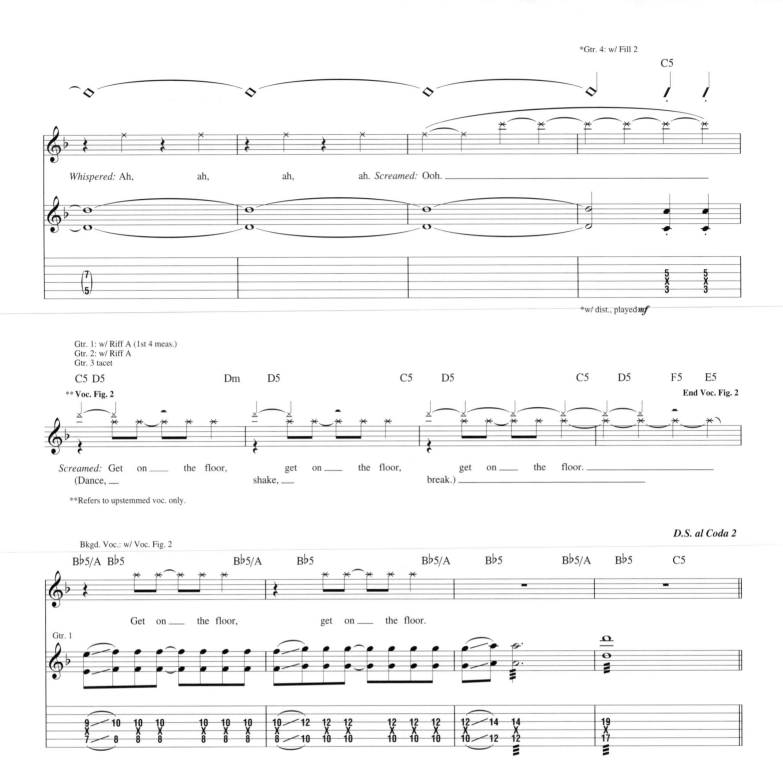

Waiting

Words and Music by Ronnie Winter

*Chord symbols reflect overall harmony.

**Vol. swell

13

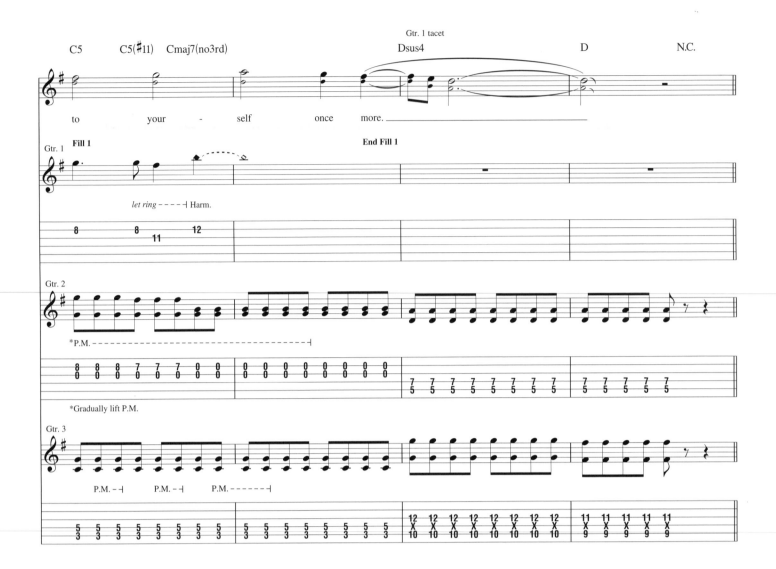

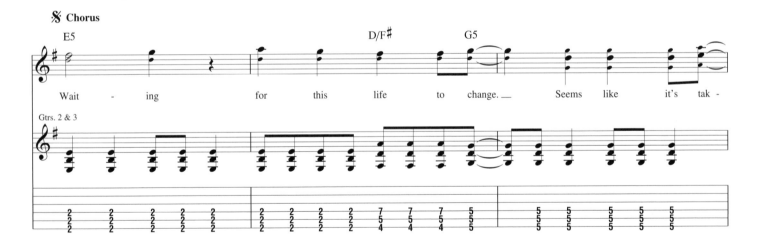

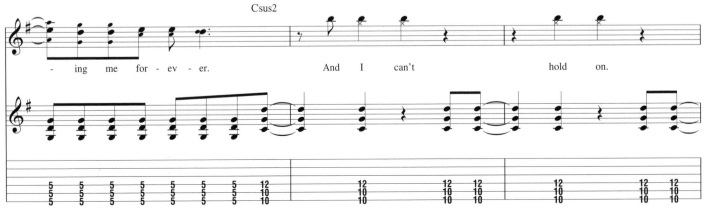

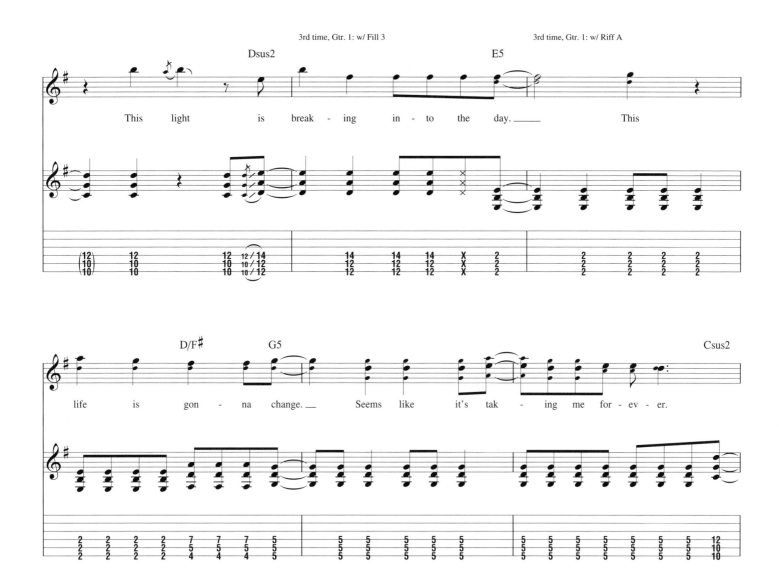

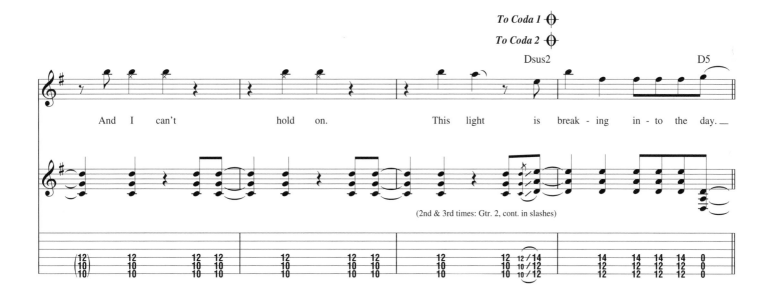

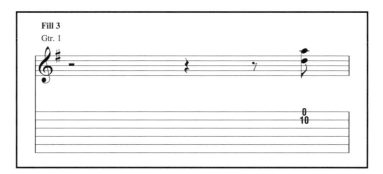

15

Interlude

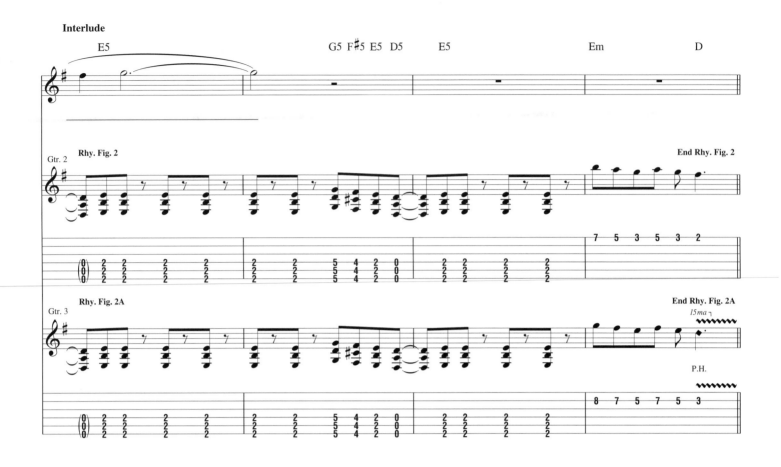

Verse

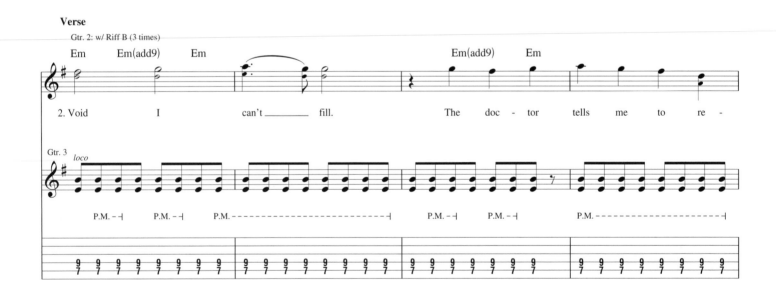

2. Void   I   can't _____ fill.   The doc - tor tells me to re -

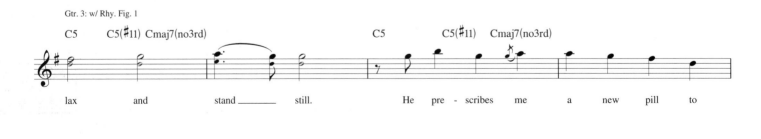

lax   and   stand _____ still.   He pre - scribes me a new pill to

quell   my   an - ger.   Wish I could make her pull her -

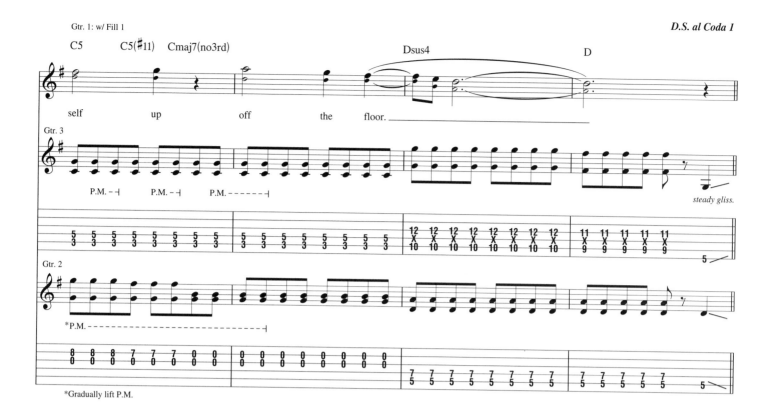

⊕ Coda 1

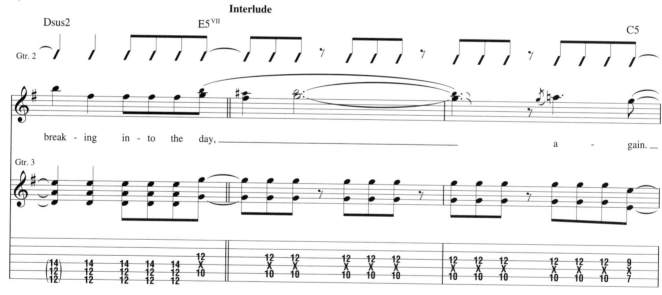

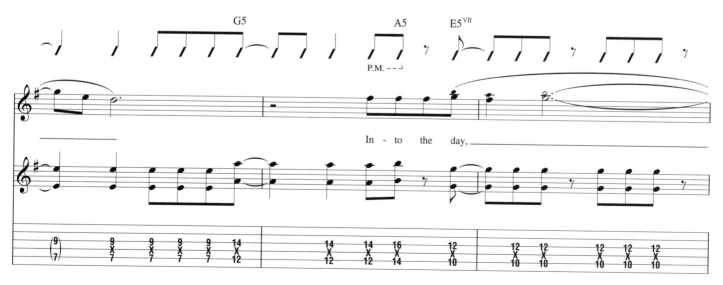

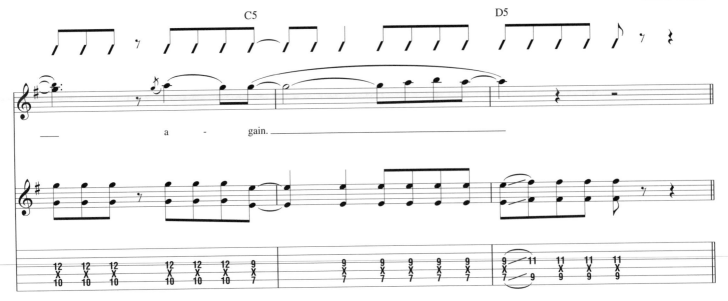

a - gain.

Coda 2

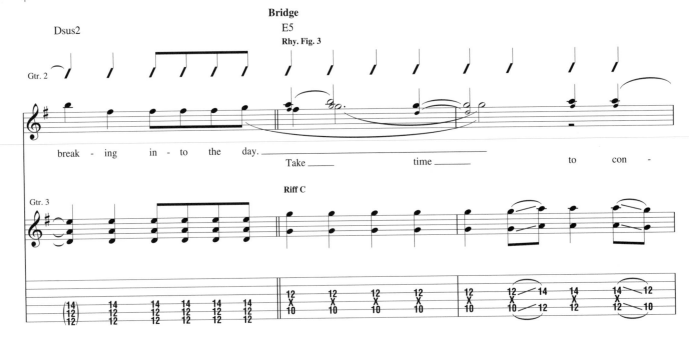

Dsus2

Bridge
E5
Rhy. Fig. 3

Gtr. 2

break - ing in - to the day. Take _____ time _____ to con -

Gtr. 3

Riff C

G5

C5

End Rhy. Fig. 3

- tem - plate _____ who you are _____ and where _____

End Riff C

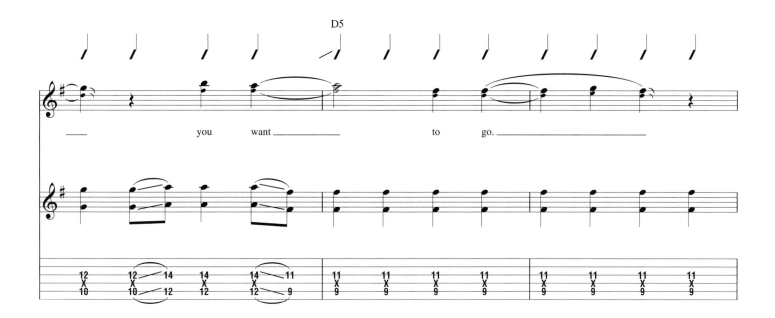

you want ____ to go. ____

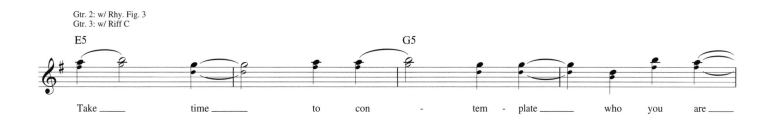

Gtr. 2: w/ Rhy. Fig. 3
Gtr. 3: w/ Riff C

Take ____ time ____ to con - tem - plate ____ who you are ____

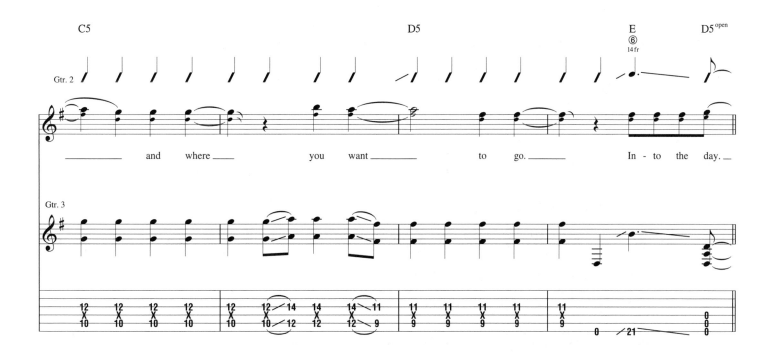

____ and where ____ you want ____ to go. ____ In - to the day. ____

Outro

Gtrs. 2 & 3: w/ Rhy. Figs. 2 & 2A

False Pretense

Words and Music by Ronnie Winter

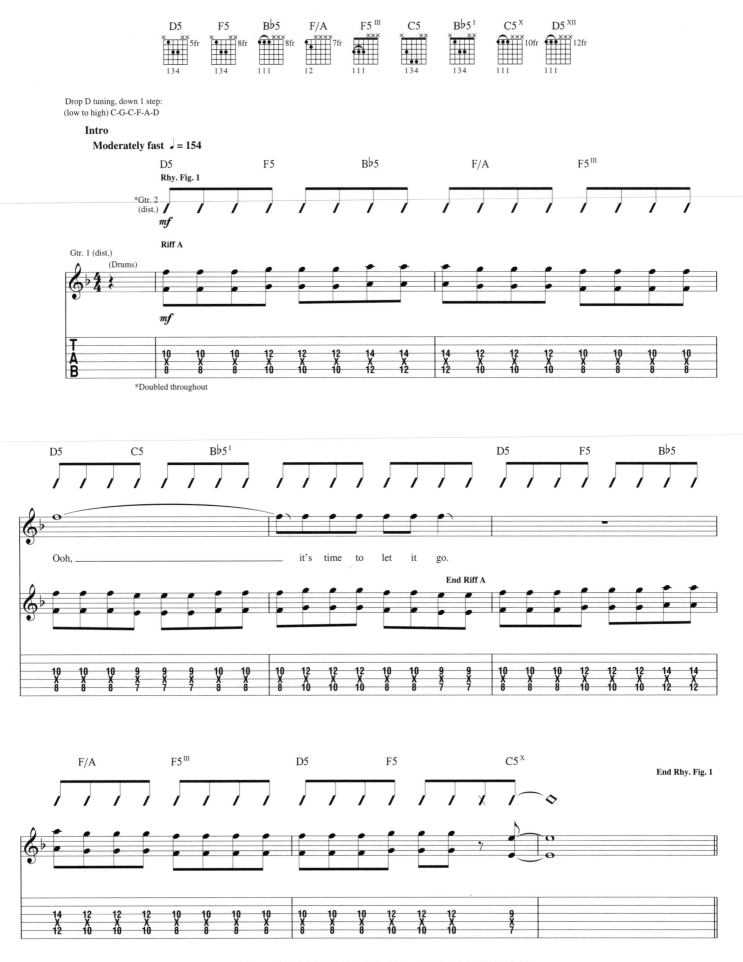

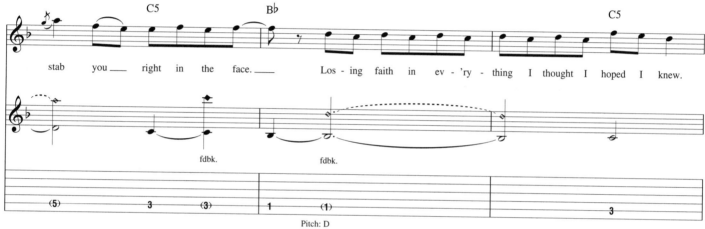

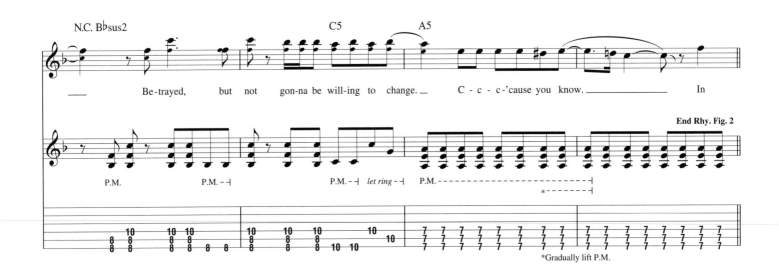

To Coda 2 ⊕

To Coda 1 ⊕

𝄋 Chorus

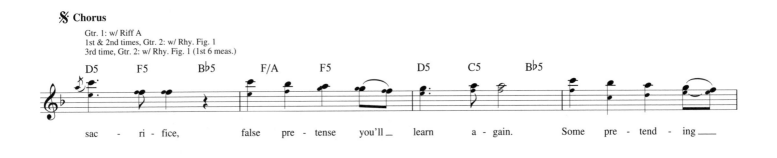

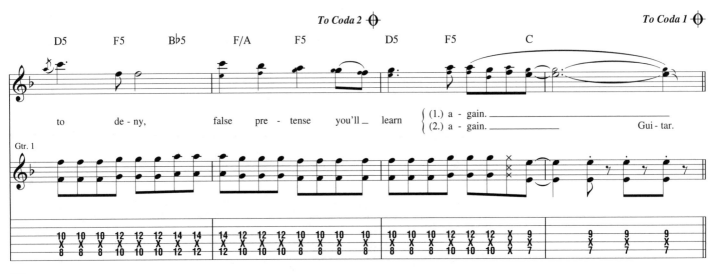

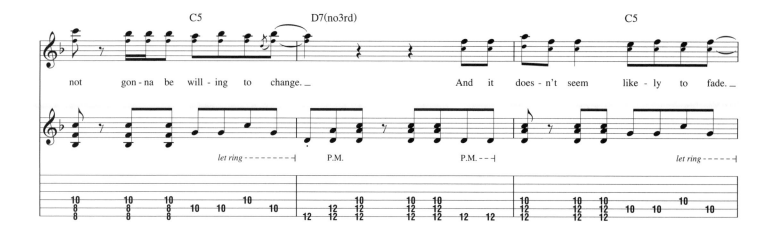

not gon-na be will-ing to change.___ And it does-n't seem like-ly to fade.___

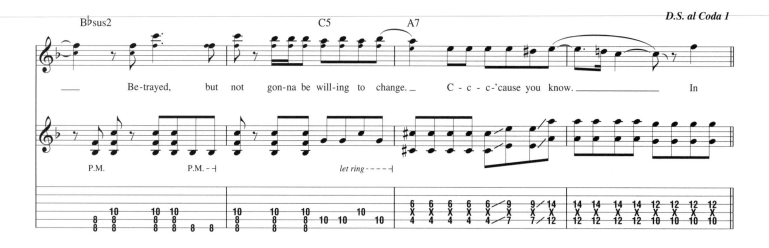

___ Be-trayed, but not gon-na be will-ing to change.___ C- c- c-'cause you know._____ In

D.S. al Coda 1

Coda 1

Ooh, _____ it's time to let it go.

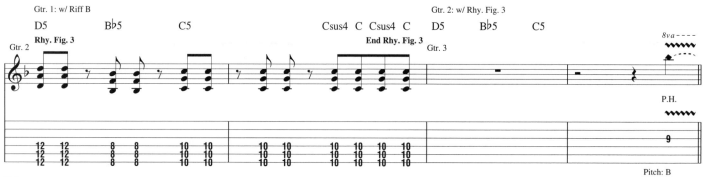

*Set appox. for quarter-note regeneration w/ 4 repeats.

D.S. al Coda 2

⊕ Coda 2

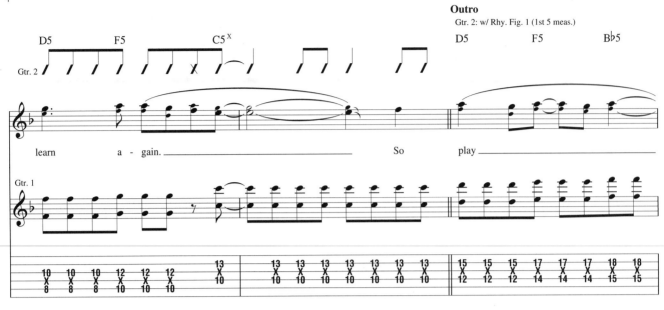

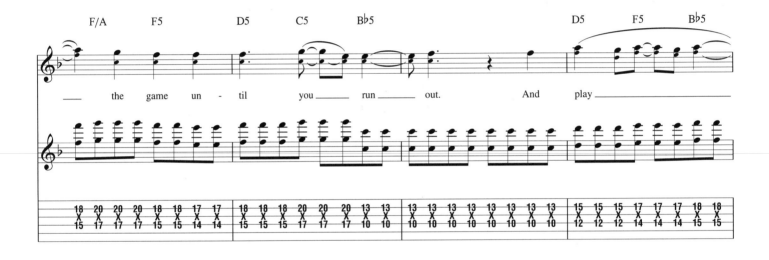

Face Down

Words and Music by Ronnie Winter

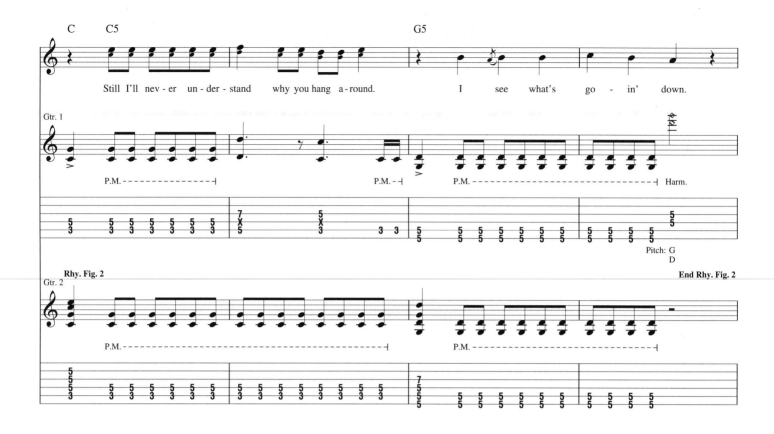

Still I'll nev-er un-der-stand   why you hang a-round.   I   see what's   go - in' down.

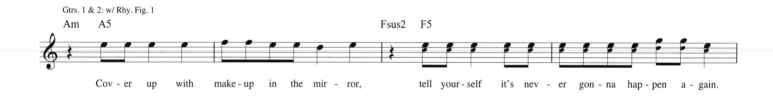

Gtrs. 1 & 2: w/ Rhy. Fig. 1

Am   A5   Fsus2   F5

Cov- er   up   with   make-up   in   the   mir-ror,   tell   your-self   it's   nev-er   gon-na   hap-pen   a-gain.

You   cry   a - lone   and   then   he   swears __ he   loves   you. ___

Chorus 𝄋

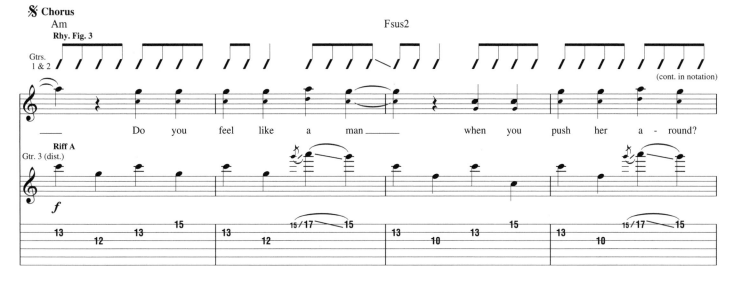

Do you feel like a man _____ when you push her a - round?

Do you feel _____ bet - ter _____ now _____ as she falls _____ to the ground? _____

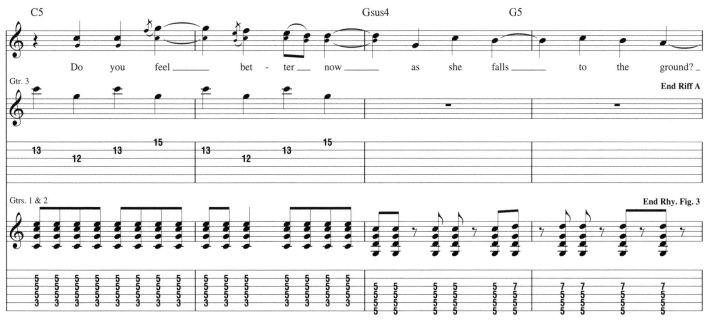

Gtrs. 1 & 2: w/ Rhy. Fig. 3
Gtr. 3: w/ Riff A

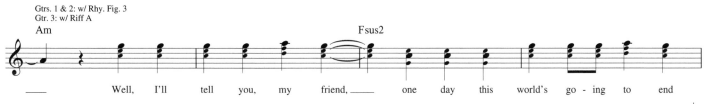

_____ Well, I'll tell you, my friend, _____ one day this world's go - ing to end

To Coda 1 ⊕

To Coda 2 ⊕

as your lies _____ crum - ble _____ down. _____ A new life _____ she has

Half-time feel   **End Half-time feel**

found. _____

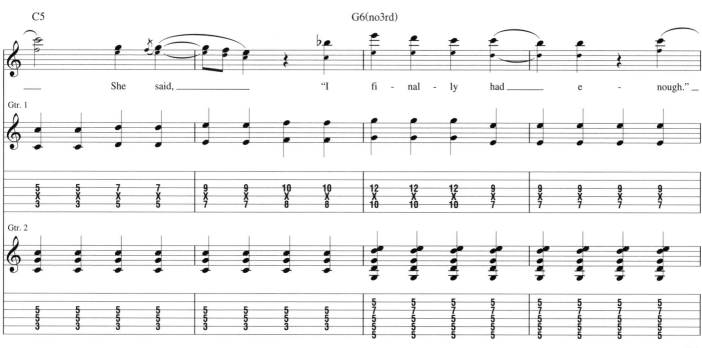

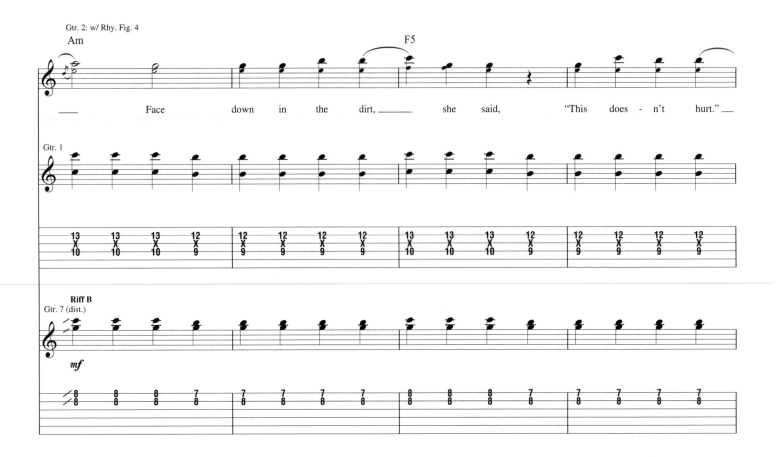

Gtr. 2: w/ Rhy. Fig. 4

Face down in the dirt, _____ she said, "This does - n't hurt." _____

She said, _____ "I fi - nal - ly had _____ e - nough." _____

Outro
Half-time feel
Gtr. 7: w/ Riff B

found.   Face   down   in   the   dirt, _____   she   said,   "This   does - n't   hurt." ____

Gtr. 1

Gtr. 2

_____   She   said, _____   "I've   fi - nal - ly   had _____   e -   nough." _

Am

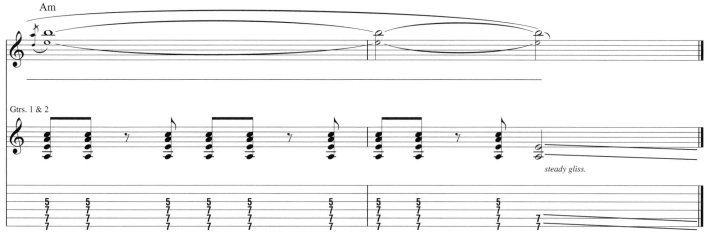

Gtrs. 1 & 2

steady gliss.

Misery Loves Its Company

Words and Music by Ronnie Winter

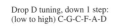

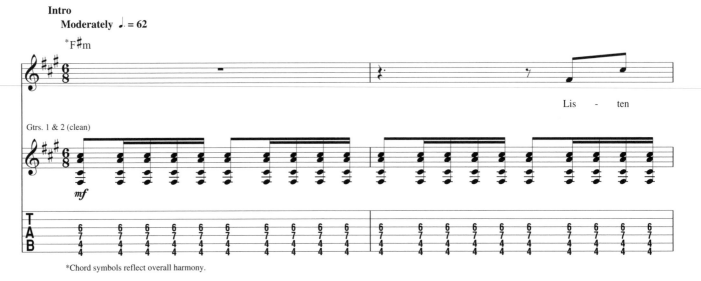

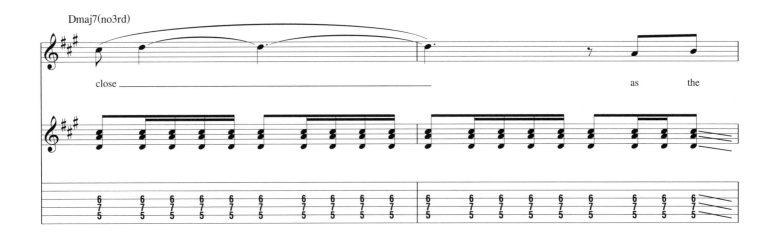

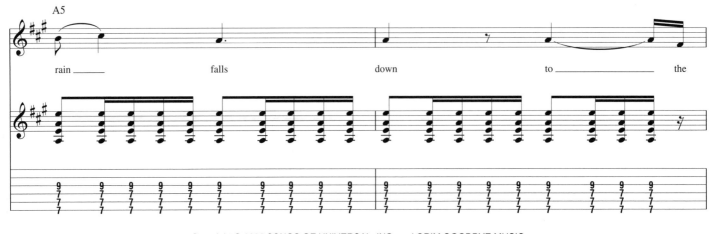

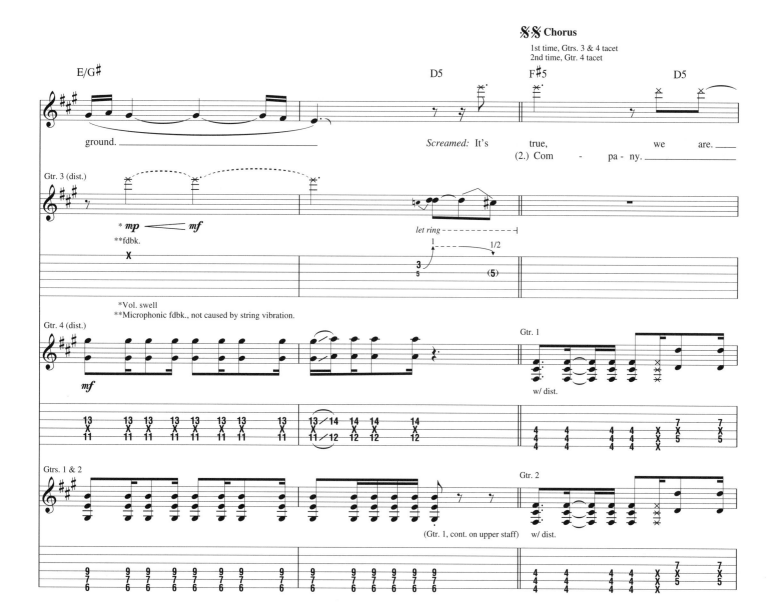

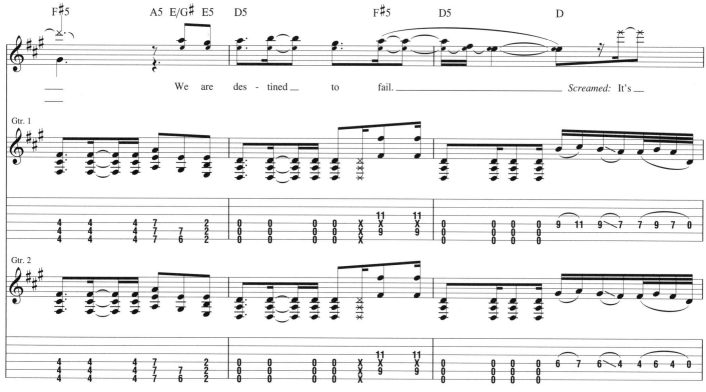

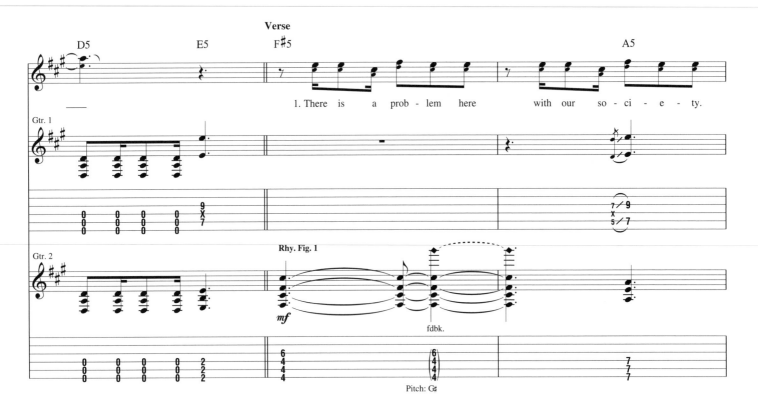

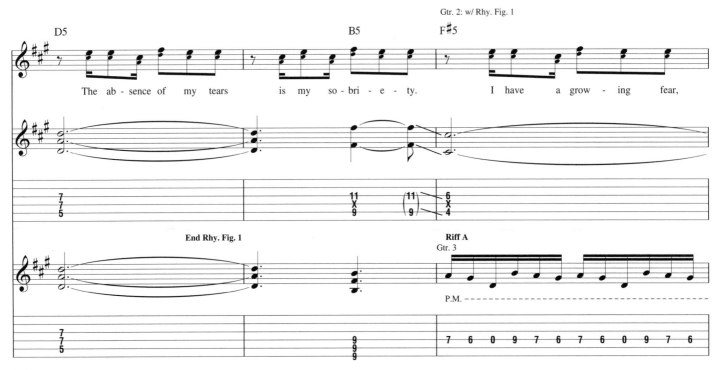

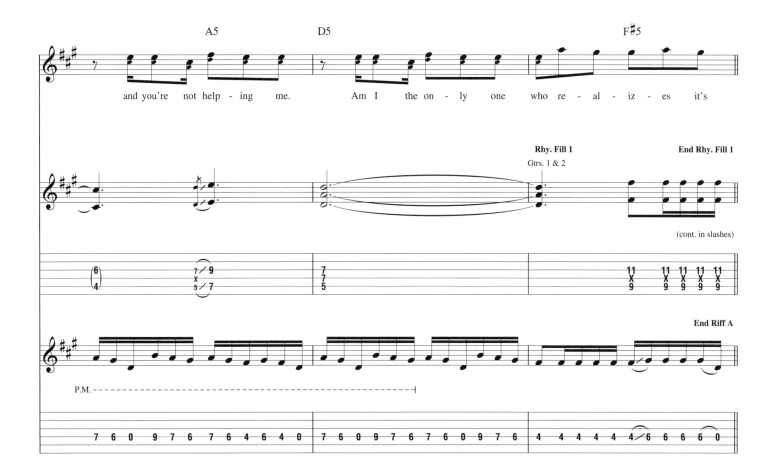

and you're not help - ing me. Am I the on - ly one who re - al - iz - es it's

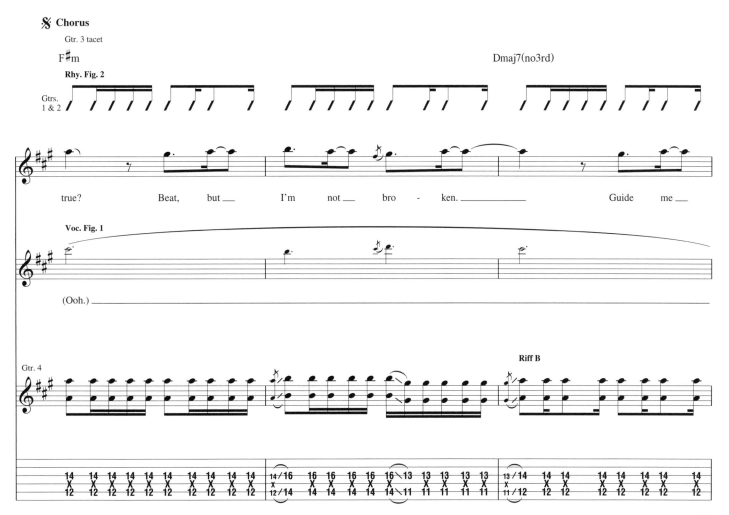

Chorus

true? Beat, but __ I'm not __ bro - ken. ____ Guide me __

(Ooh.) _____

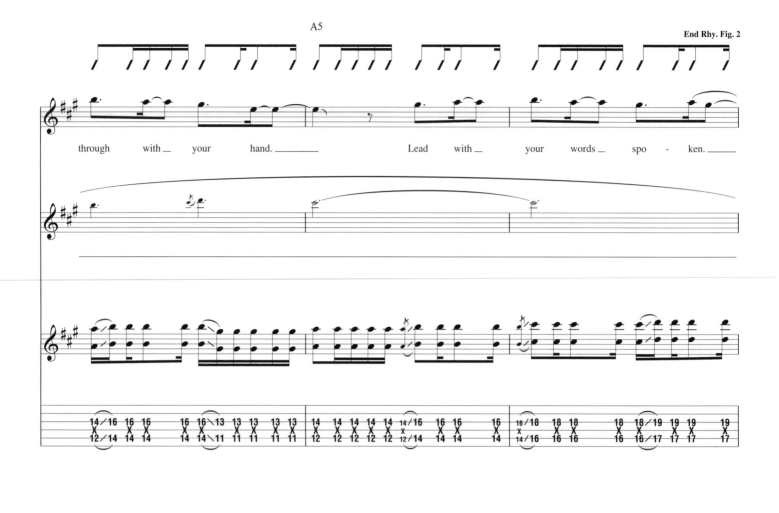

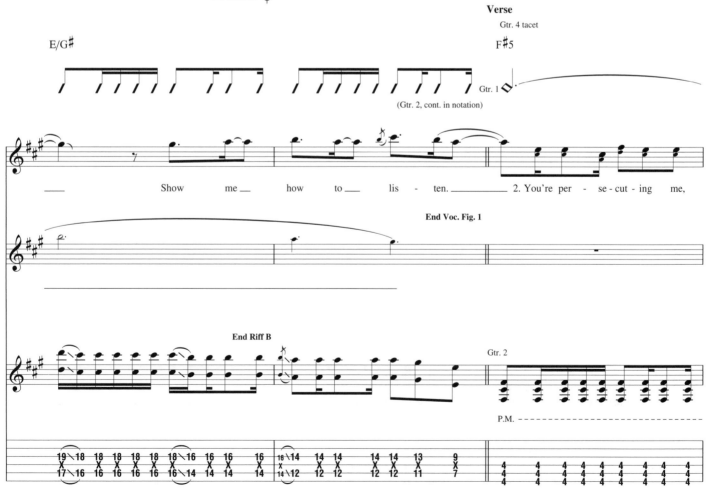

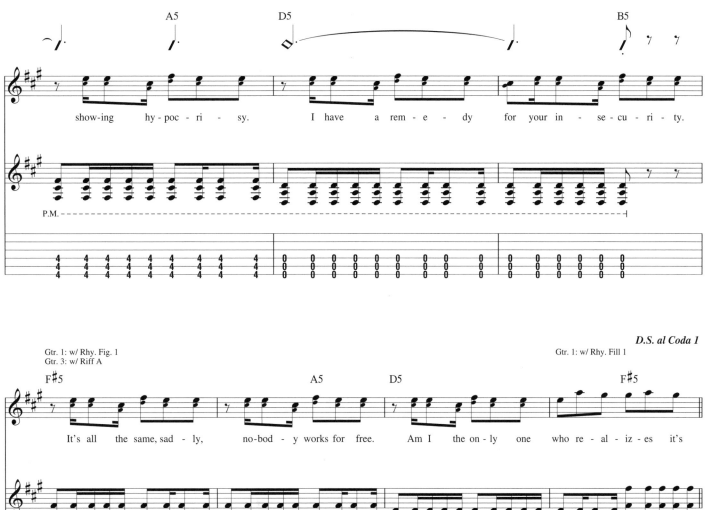

showing hy-poc-ri-sy. I have a rem-e-dy for your in-se-cu-ri-ty.

Gtr. 1: w/ Rhy. Fig. 1
Gtr. 3: w/ Riff A

D.S. al Coda 1

Gtr. 1: w/ Rhy. Fill 1

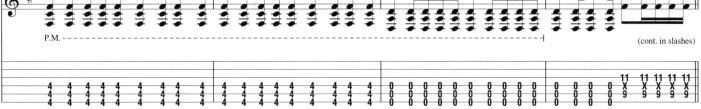

It's all the same, sad-ly, no-bod-y works for free. Am I the on-ly one who re-al-iz-es it's

Coda 1

Bkgd. Voc.: w/ Voc. Fig. 1 (last meas.)
Bkgd. Voc.: w/ Voc. Fig. 1
Gtrs. 1 & 2: w/ Rhy. Fig. 2 (1st 5 meas.)

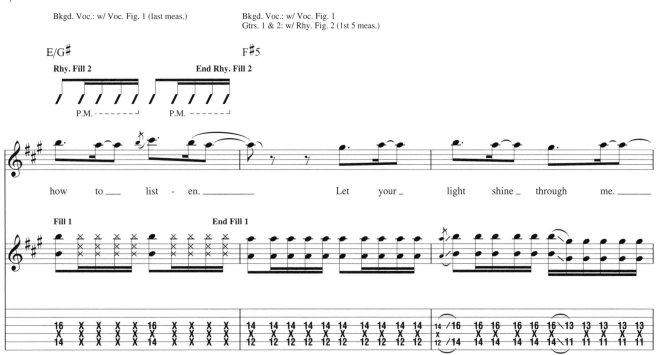

how to list-en. Let your light shine through me.

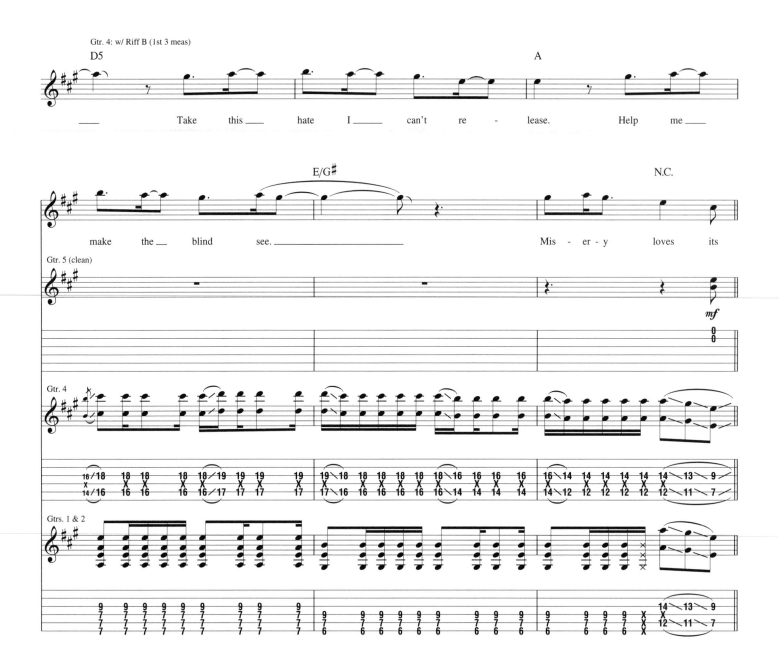

Gtr. 4: w/ Riff B (1st 3 meas)

Take this ___ hate I ___ can't re - lease. Help me ___

make the ___ blind see. ___ Mis - er - y loves its

Gtr. 5 (clean)

Gtr. 4

Gtrs. 1 & 2

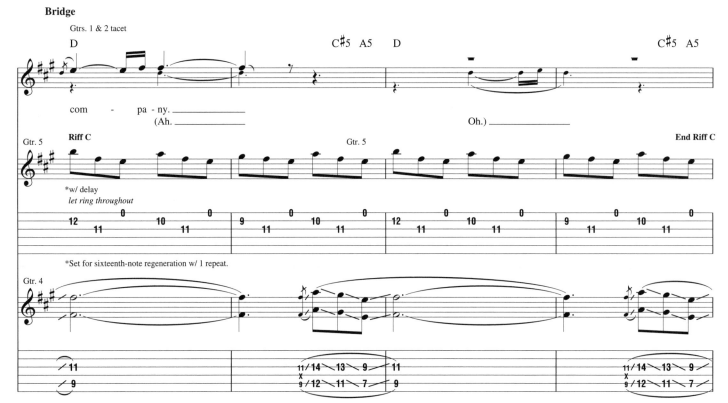

Bridge

Gtrs. 1 & 2 tacet

com - pa - ny. ___
(Ah. ___) Oh.) ___

Gtr. 5   **Riff C**   Gtr. 5   **End Riff C**

*w/ delay
let ring throughout

*Set for sixteenth-note regeneration w/ 1 repeat.

Gtr. 4

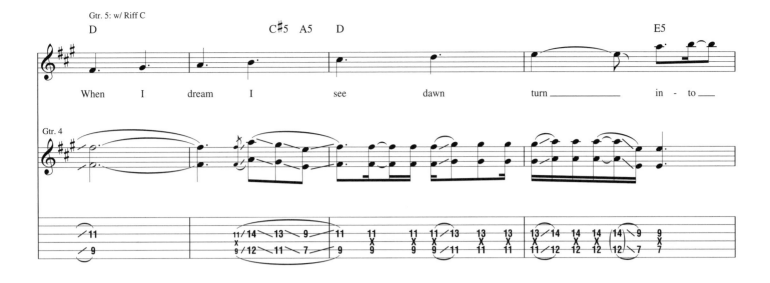

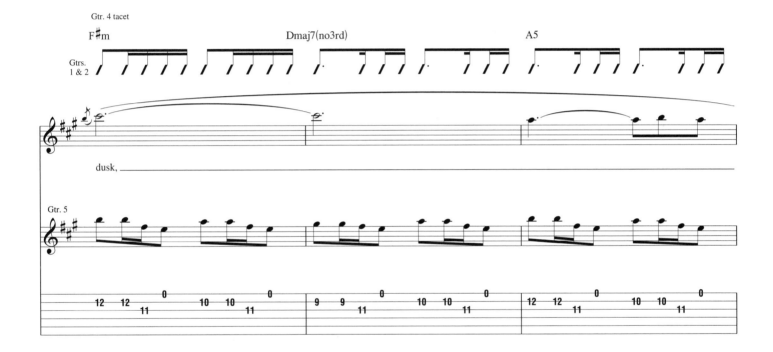

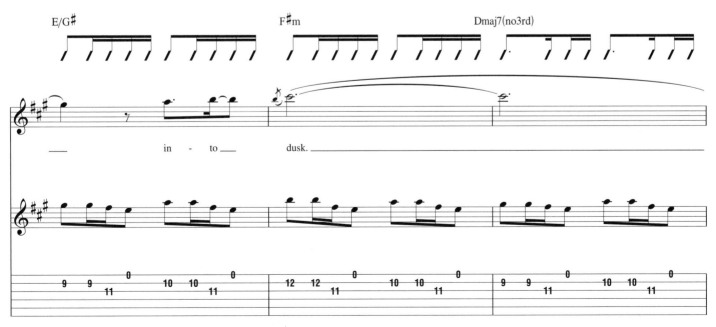

44

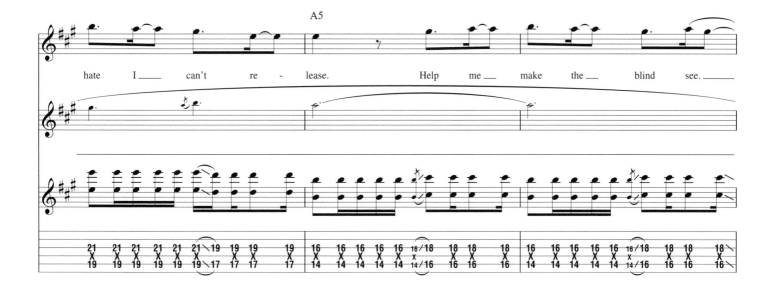

hate I ____ can't re - lease. Help me ___ make the ___ blind see. ___

D.S.S. al Coda 2

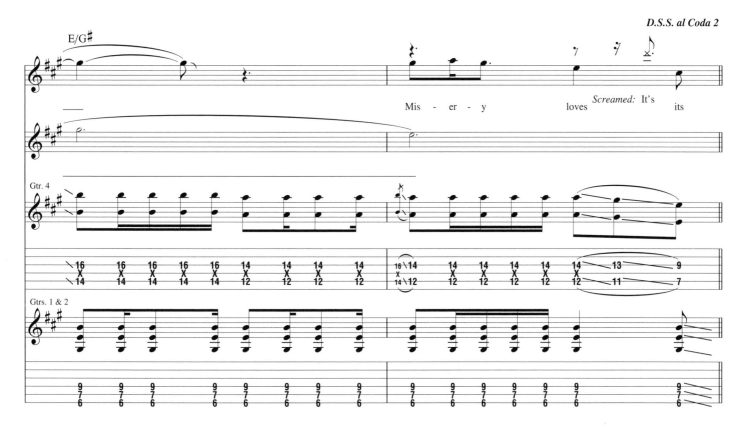

Mis - er - y loves *Screamed:* It's its

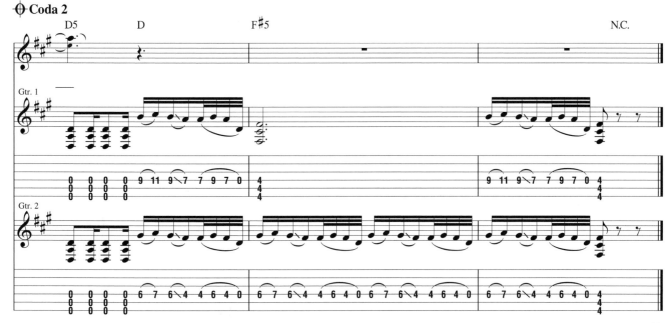

Cat and Mouse

Words and Music by Ronnie Winter

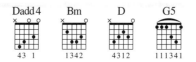

Gtr. 1: Drop D tuning, down 1 step:
(low to high) C-G-C-F-A-D
Gtrs. 2 & 3: Double drop D tuning, down 1 step:
(low to high) C-G-C-F-A-C

Intro

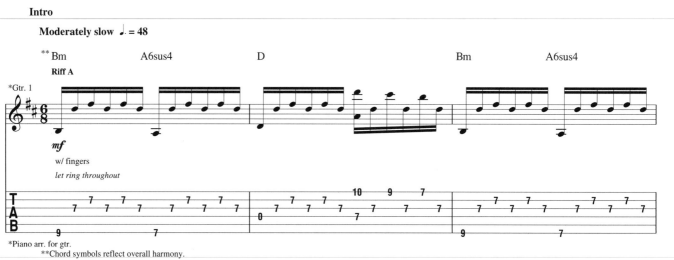

*Piano arr. for gtr.
**Chord symbols reflect overall harmony.

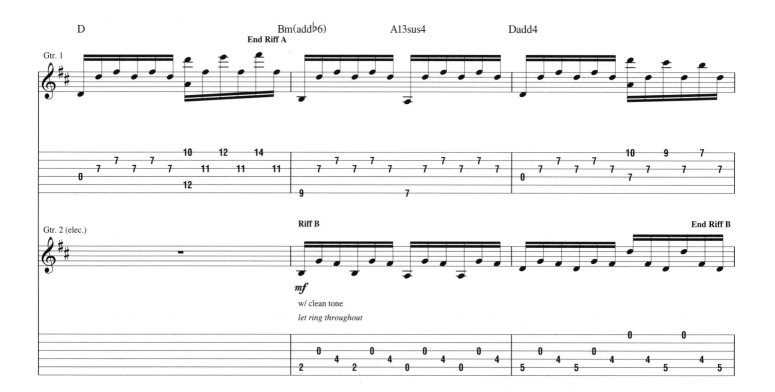

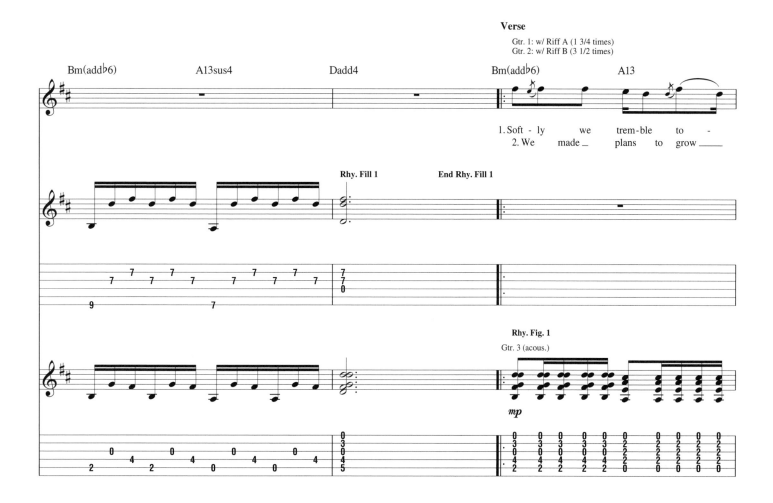

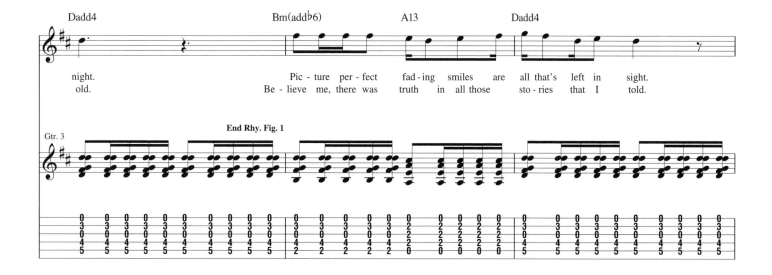

% Chorus

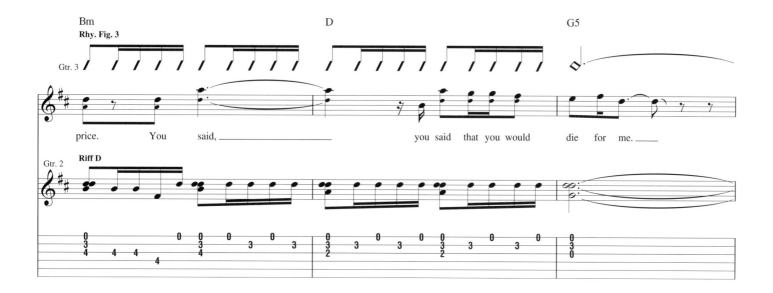

price. You said, _____ you said that you would die for me. _____

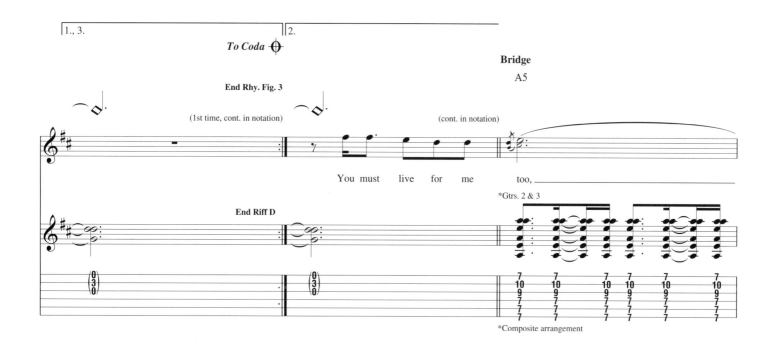

You must live for me too, _____

*Gtrs. 2 & 3

*Composite arrangement

for me too, _____ yeah, _____ yeah,

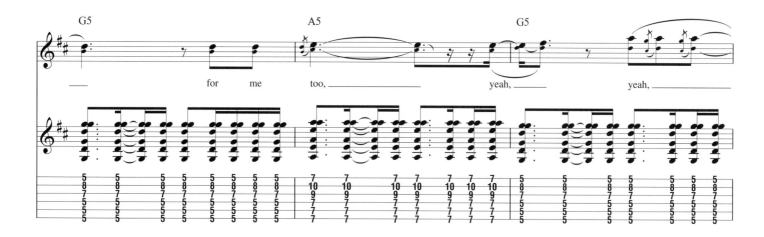

Gtr. 2: w/ Riff C
Gtr. 3: w/ Rhy. Fig. 2

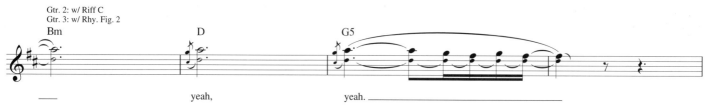

___ yeah, _____ yeah. _____

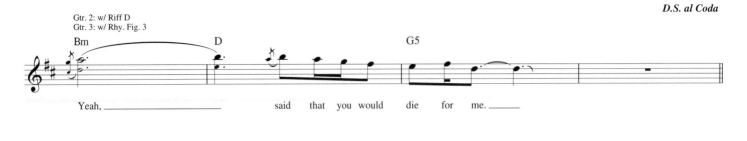

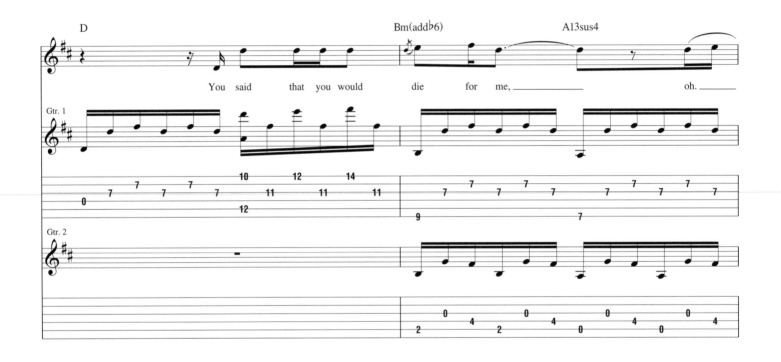

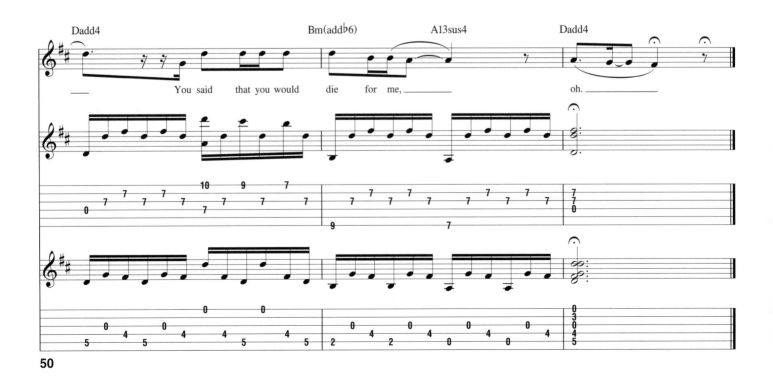

Damn Regret

Words and Music by Ronnie Winter

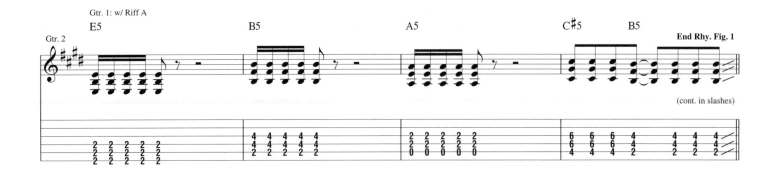

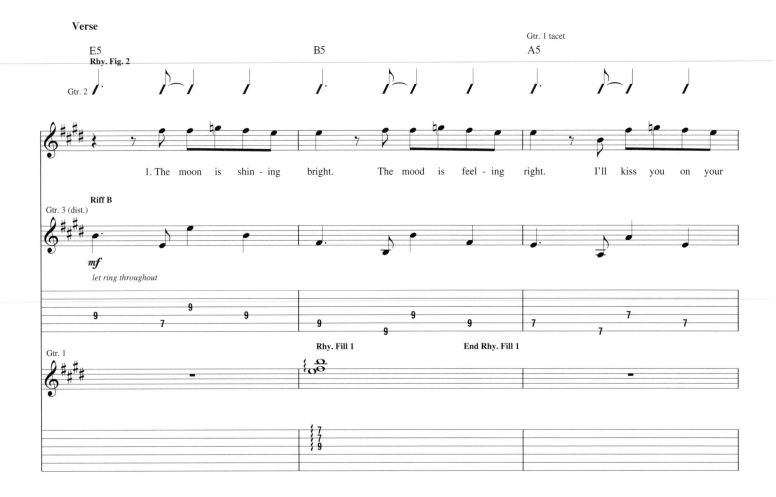

52

found. Em - pow - ered by a - dren - a - line, feel I've been born a - gain. A - gain I am re -

peat - ing my - self. ___ And I _____ know _ when it's time ___ for you to sit and 1. pre - tend. ___ 2. pre -

Chorus

1st time, Gtr. 1: w/ Riff A (2 times)
1st time, Gtr. 2: w/ Rhy. Fig. 1
2nd time, Gtr. 1: w/ Riff A (1 3/4 times)
2nd time, Gtr. 2: w/ Rhy. Fig. 1 (1st 7 meas.)

tend. Damn re - gret. I'll try to for - get. ___ Don't wor - ry a - bout ___ me 'cause I'm ___ re - fined. ___

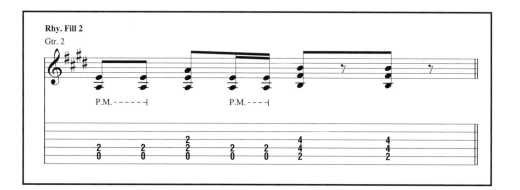

Atrophy

Words and Music by Ronnie Winter

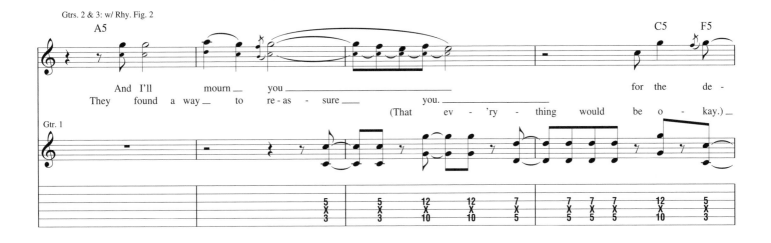

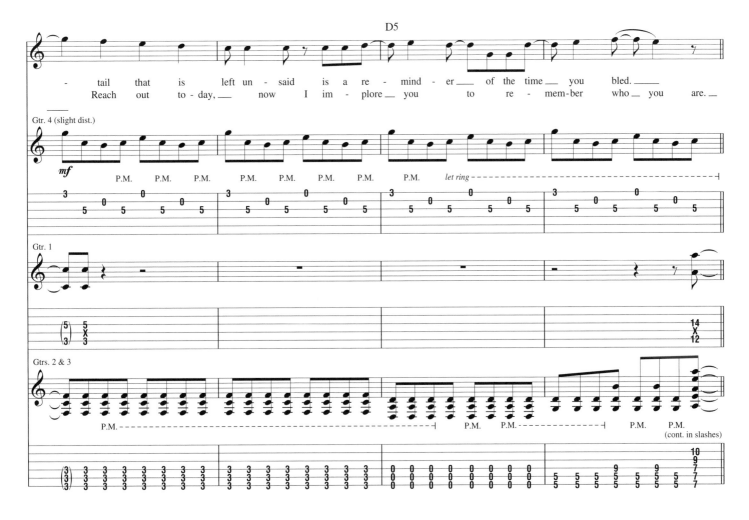

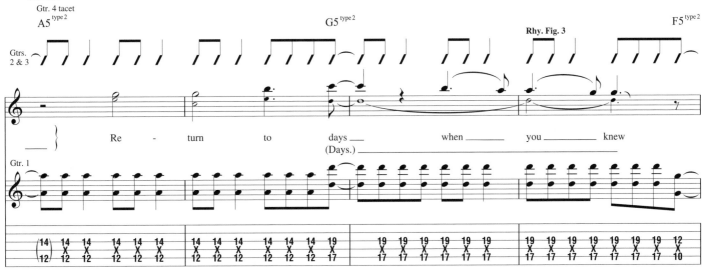

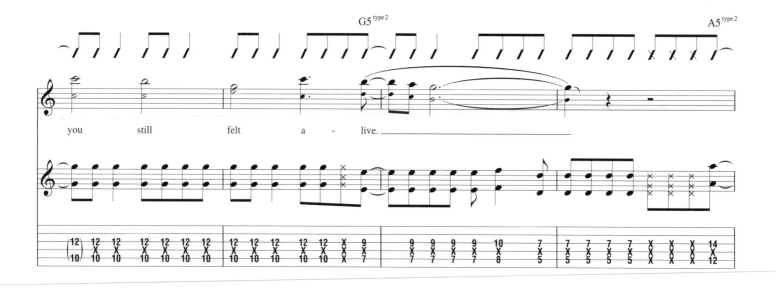

you still felt a - live. _____

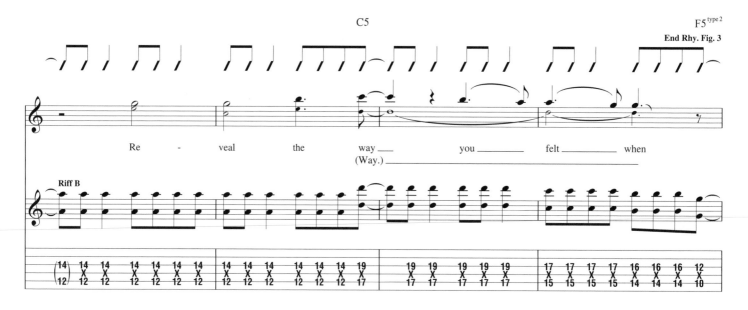

Re - veal the way ____ you ____ felt ____ when
(Way.) _____

Riff B

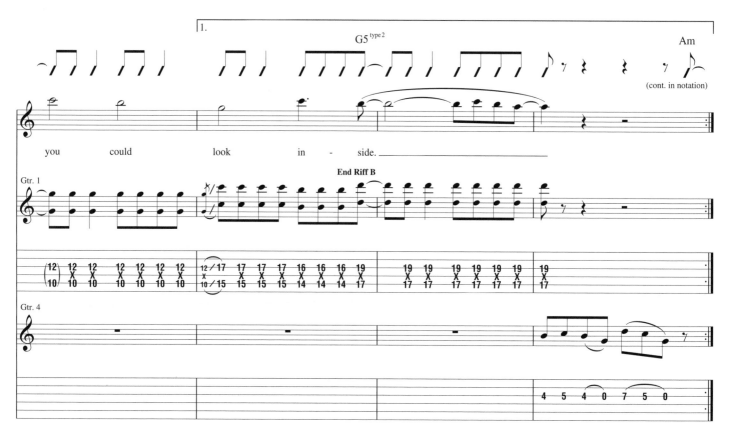

you could look in - side. _____

Gtr. 1

End Riff B

Gtr. 4

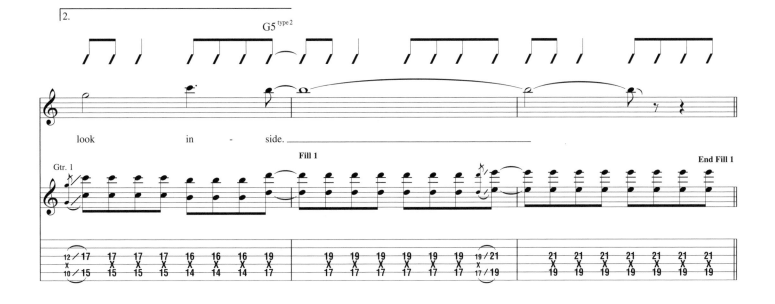

look in - side. _____

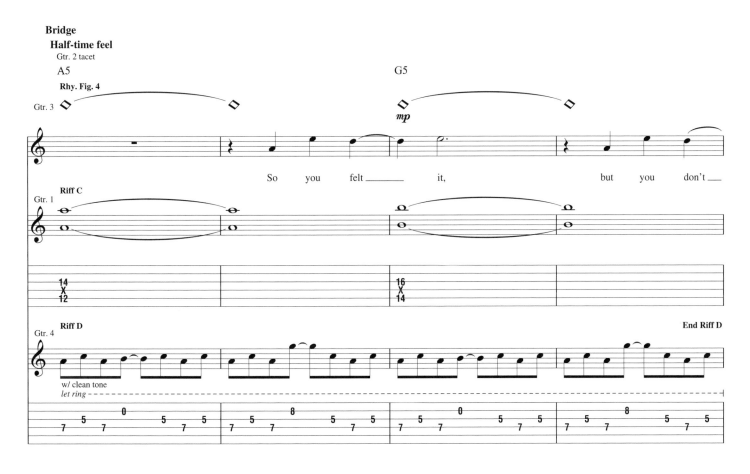

Bridge
Half-time feel
Gtr. 2 tacet

A5   G5

So you felt _____ it,   but you don't _____

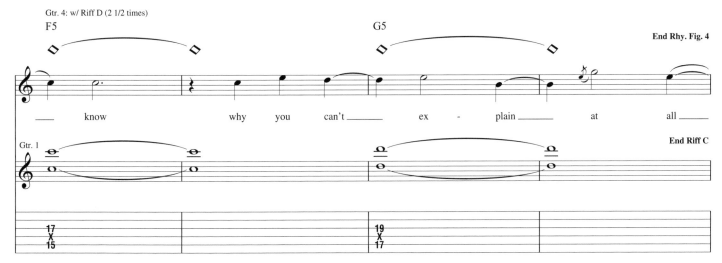

_____ know   why you can't _____ ex - plain _____ at   all _____

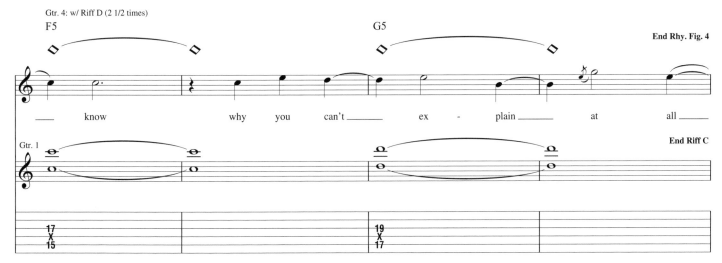

Gtr. 1: w/ Riff C
Gtr. 3: w/ Rhy. Fig. 4

*Am(add9)   Gsus²₄

_____   why you felt _____ it   'cause you don't _____

* Chord symbols reflect overall harmony.

Fadd♯¹¹⁹   Gsus²₄

_____ know,   no,   you   don't _____ know. _____

A5   G5

Gtrs.
2 & 3
mf

** Voc. Fig. 1

Break   the   walls _____ be - tween build - ing   at - ro - phy

Riff E   End Riff E
Gtr. 5 (dist.)

mf

```
|-----------------|----------------|-------|---------------|---------|
|-14--------------|-14-------12----|-16----|-16------------|-12------|
|-X---------------|-X--------X-----|-X-----|-X-------------|-X-------|
|-12--------------|-12-------10----|-14----|-14------------|-10------|
|-----------------|----------------|-------|---------------|---------|
```

**Refers to Ld. voc. only.

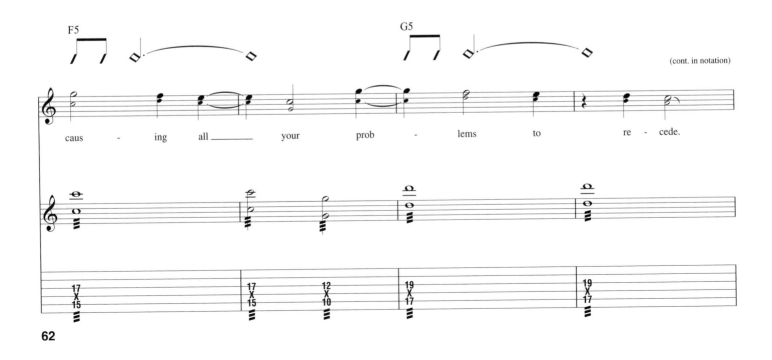

F5   G5

caus - ing   all _____ your   prob - lems   to   re - cede.

(cont. in notation)

```
|-----------------|----------------|-------|---------------|
|-17--------------|-17-------12----|-19----|-19------------|
|-X---------------|-X--------X-----|-X-----|-X-------------|
|-15--------------|-15-------10----|-17----|-17------------|
|-----------------|----------------|-------|---------------|
```

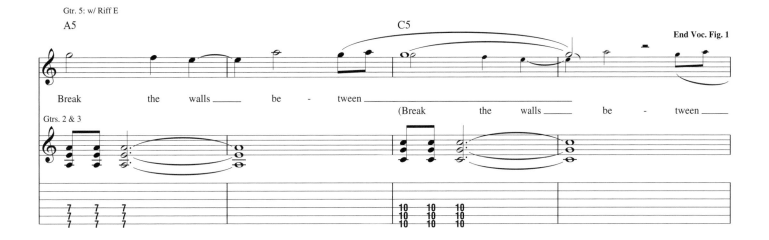

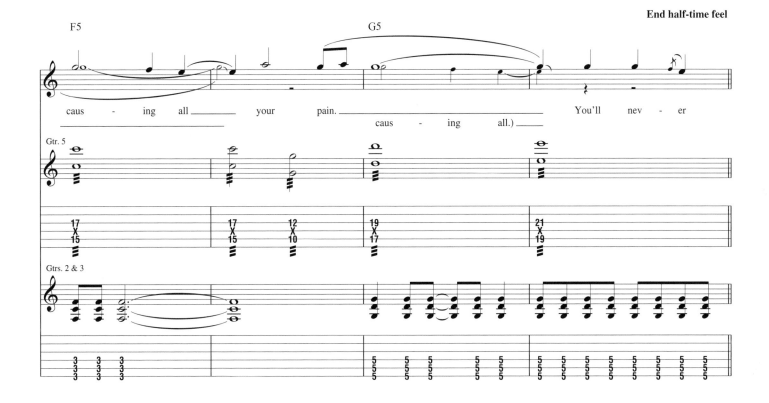

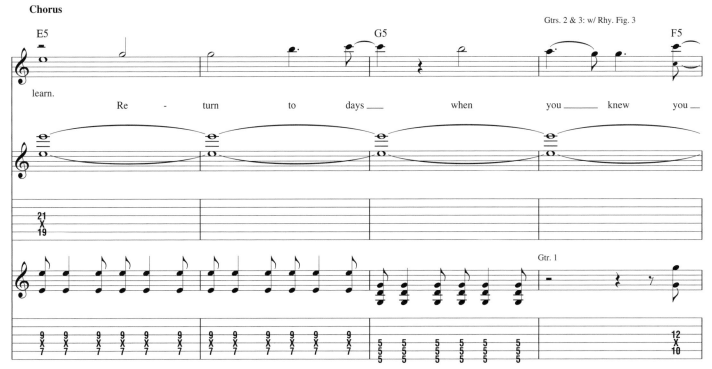

beat in your heart. When you can't be bought. __ The beat in your heart. When

you can't be bought. __ (Caus - ing all _____ your pain.) _____ The beat in your heart. Why fight when you can't be

Gtr. 1

Gtr. 5

let ring -

Outro

Gtr. 1: w/ Riff A
Gtrs. 2 & 3: w/ Rhy. Fig. 1

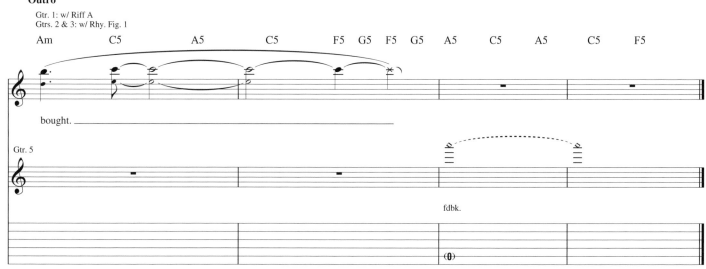

bought. _____

Gtr. 5

fdbk.

65

Seventeen Ain't So Sweet

Words and Music by Ronnie Winter

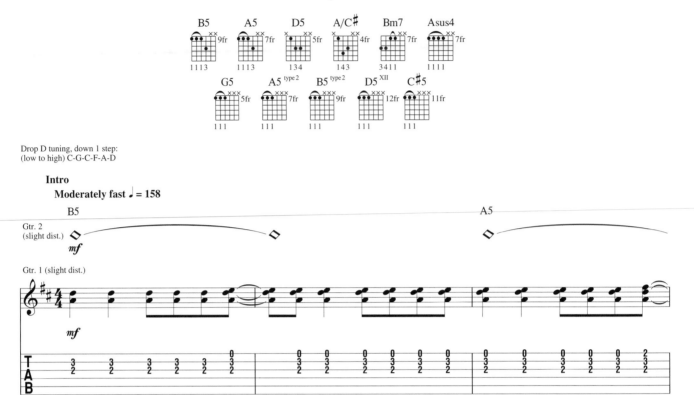

Drop D tuning, down 1 step:
(low to high) C-G-C-F-A-D

Intro

Moderately fast ♩ = 158

*Chord symbols reflect overall harmony.

yeah, at fol - low - ing ___ the ___ trends. ___ Stayed one

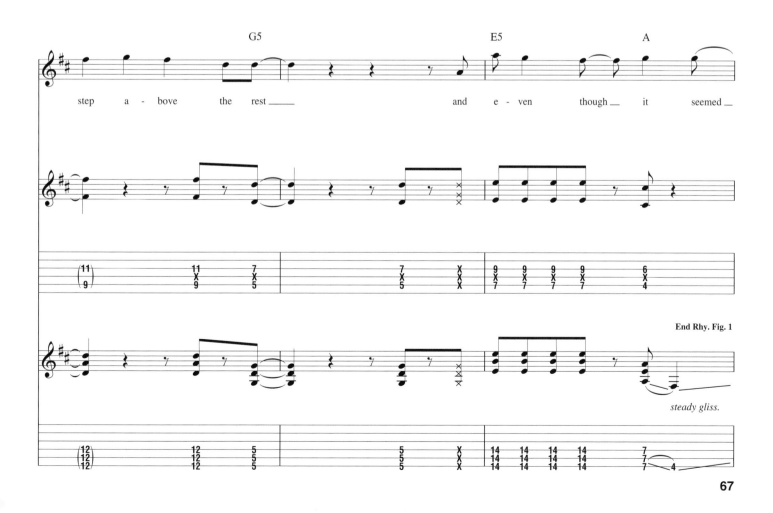

step a - bove the rest ___ and e - ven though ___ it seemed ___

End Rhy. Fig. 1

steady gliss.

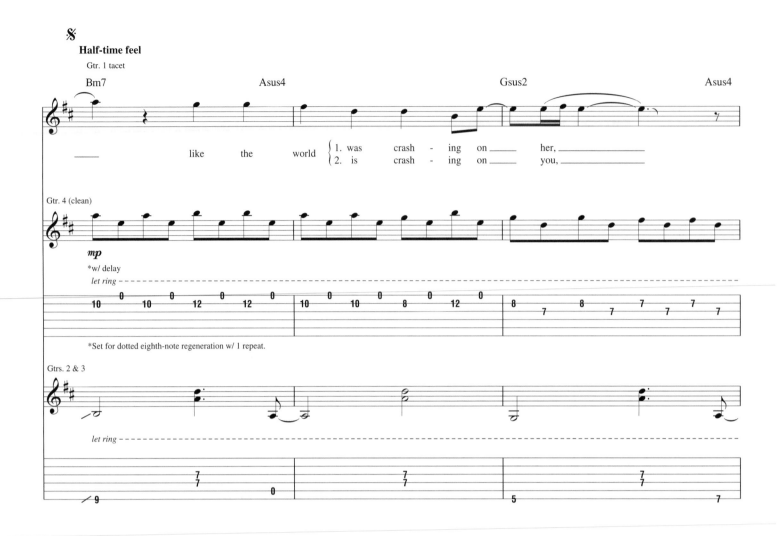

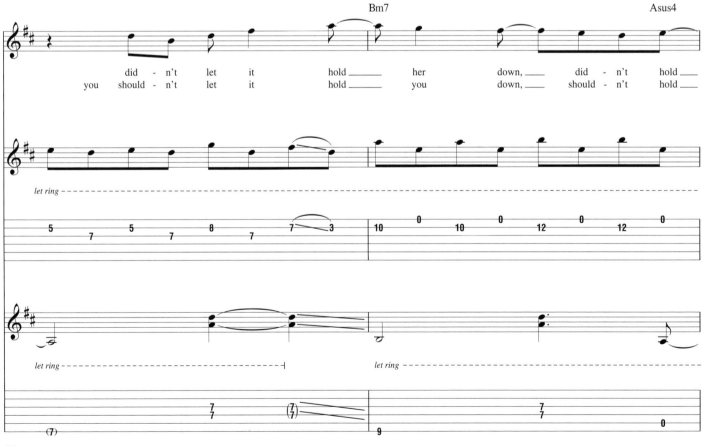

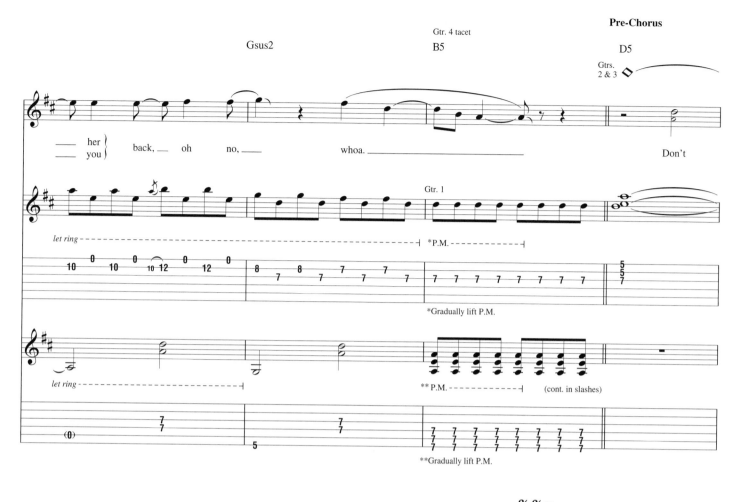

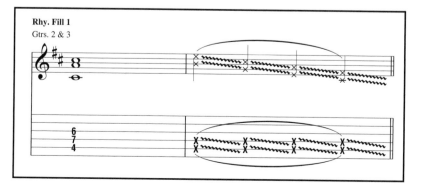

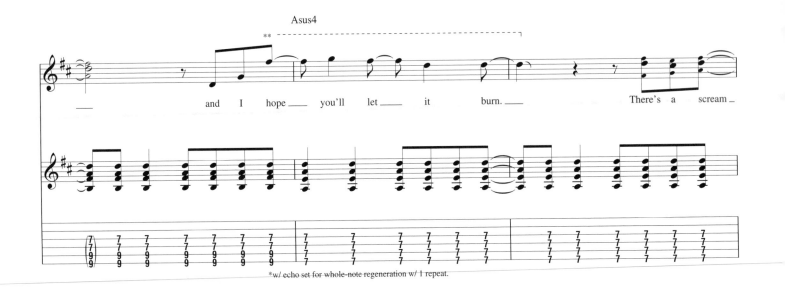

*w/ echo set for whole-note regeneration w/ 1 repeat.

**As before.

70

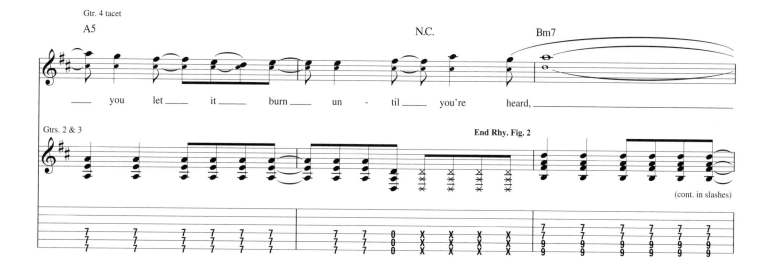

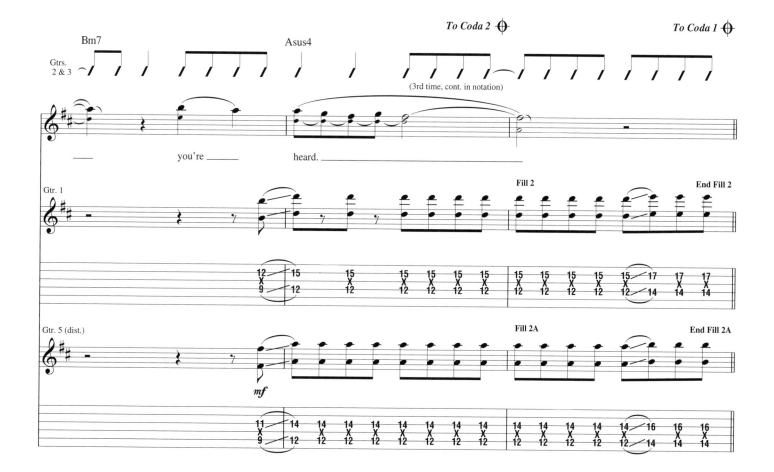

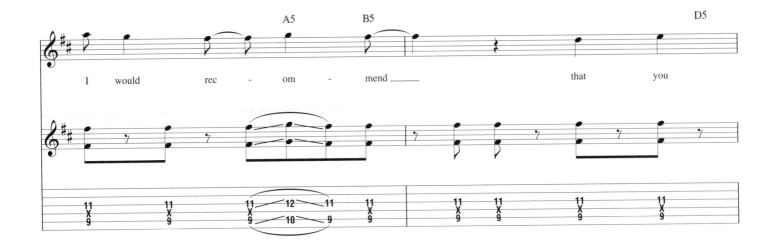

A5 B5   D5

I would rec - om - mend _____   that   you

D.S. al Coda 1

G5   E5   A5

live with no re - grets ____   e - ven if ____ it   seems ____

⊕ Coda 1

Bridge

G5   A5 type 2   End Rhy. Fig. 3

Rhy. Fig. 3

P.M. -

Re - lax, ____ girl,   turn down the lights.

Riff A

Riff A1

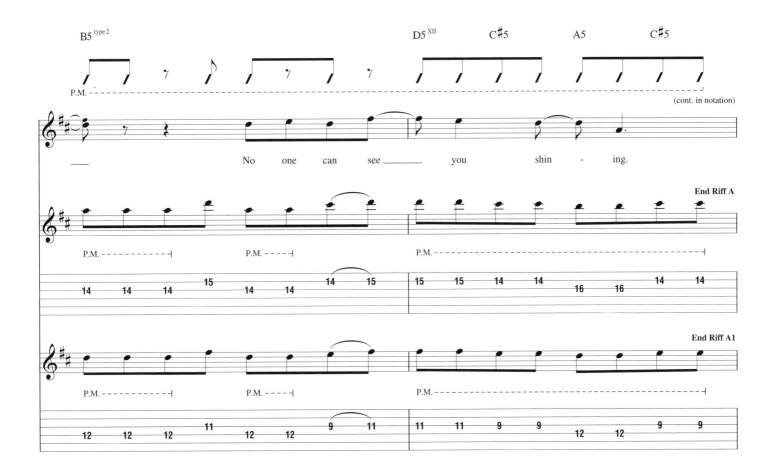

No one can see _____ you shin - ing.

End Riff A

End Riff A1

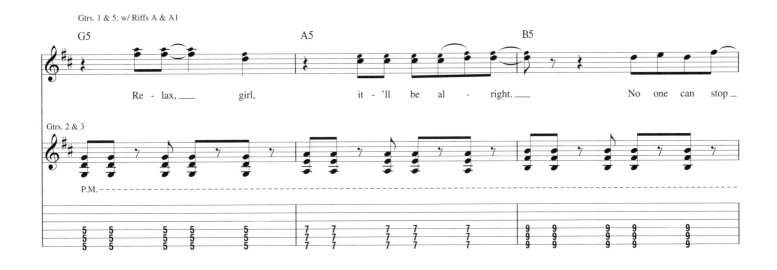

Gtrs. 1 & 5: w/ Riffs A & A1

Re - lax, ____ girl, it - 'll be al - right. ____ No one can stop ____

Gtrs. 2 & 3

Gtrs. 2 & 3: w/ Rhy. Fig. 3

____ you if ____ you try. ____ Point of rhy - thm is to fol - ow it ____ in time, ____

Gtr. 1

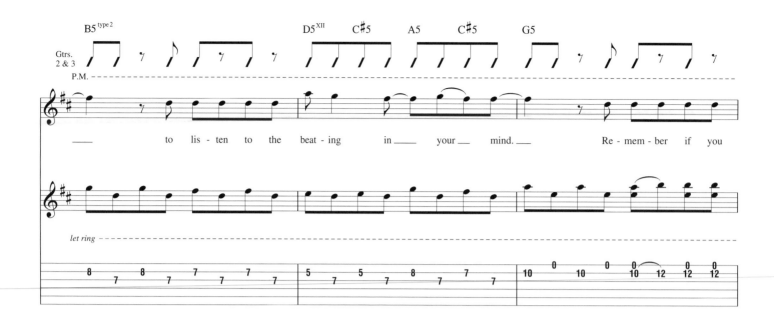

to lis-ten to the beat-ing in ___ your ___ mind. ___ Re-mem-ber if you

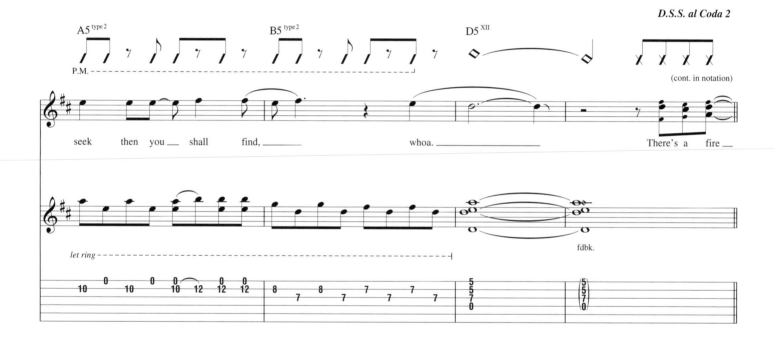

seek then you ___ shall find, _____ whoa. _____ There's a fire ___

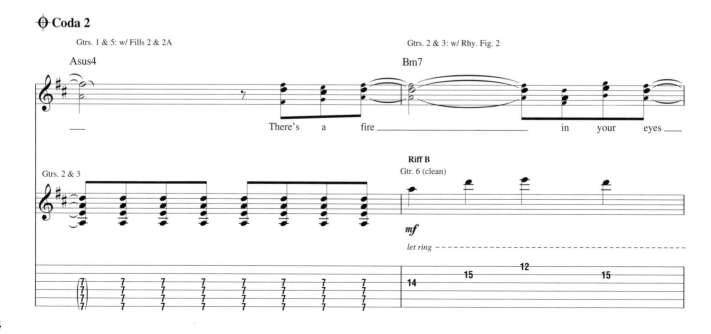

There's a fire _____ in your eyes ___

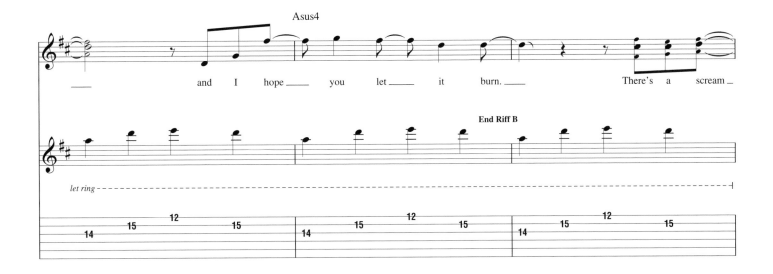

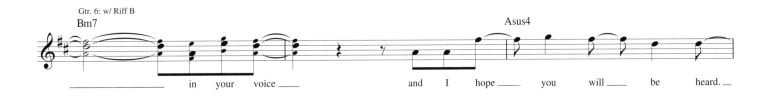

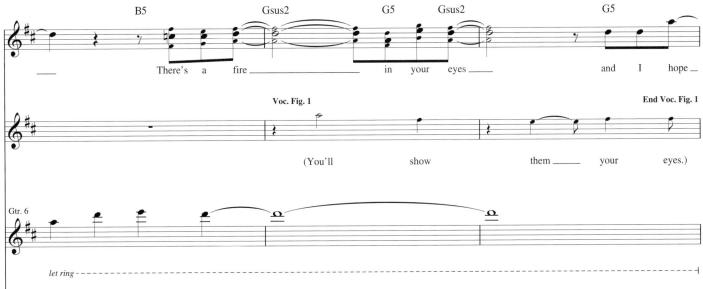

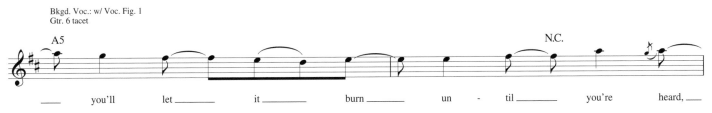

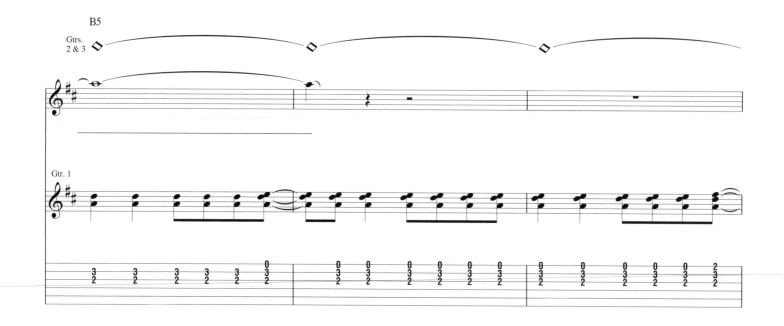

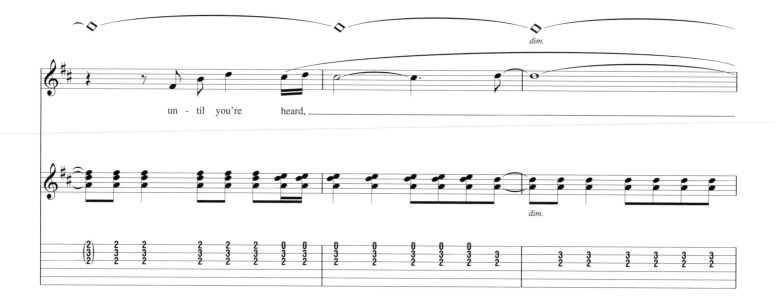

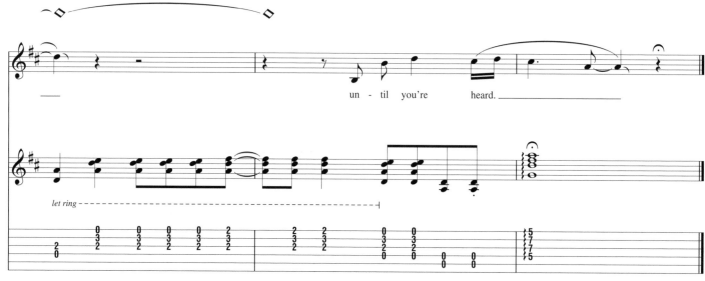

Justify

Words and Music by Ronnie Winter

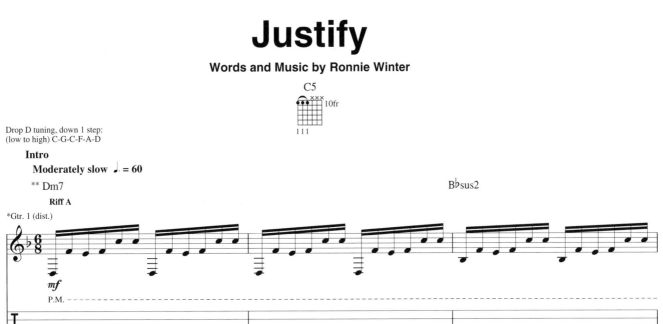

Drop D tuning, down 1 step:
(low to high) C-G-C-F-A-D

Intro

Moderately slow ♩ = 60

*Doubled throughout

**Chord symbols reflect implied harmony.

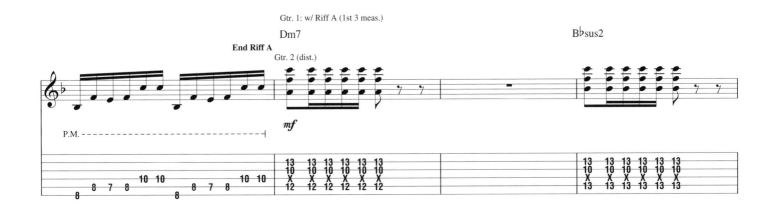

Gtr. 1: w/ Riff A (1st 3 meas.)

Verse

Gtr. 1: w/ Riff A (2 times)
Gtr. 2 tacet
2nd time, Gtr. 4 tacet

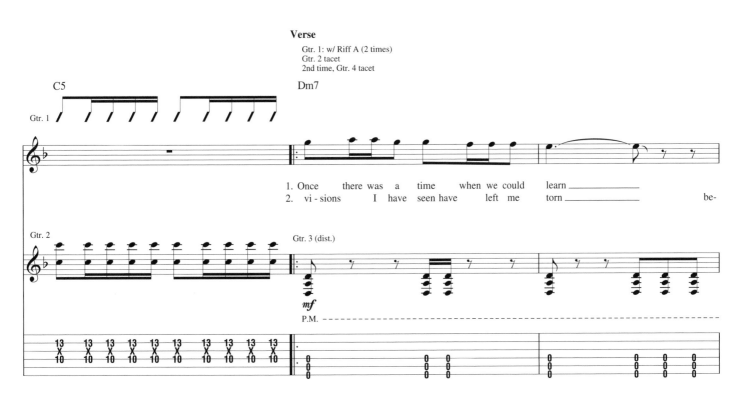

1. Once there was a time when we could learn _____
2. vi - sions I have seen have left me torn _____ be-

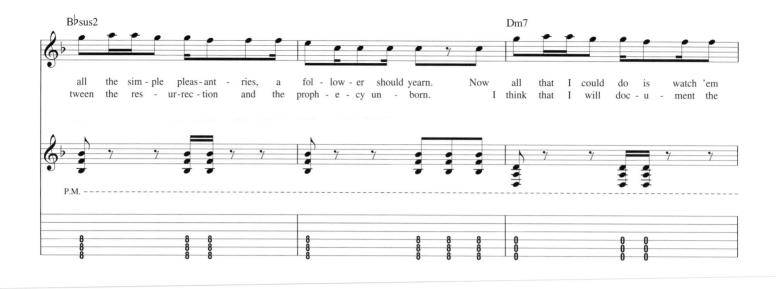

all the sim - ple pleas-ant - ries, a fol - low - er should yearn. Now all that I could do is watch 'em
tween the res - ur-rec - tion and the proph - e - cy un - born. I think that I will doc - u - ment the

Pre-Chorus

Gtr. 3 tacet

burn and wish that I could save 'em all, ___ (or) just one. ___ *Screamed:* See the
fall and say I hate to say it, but I told you all. ___

Riff B
Gtr. 1

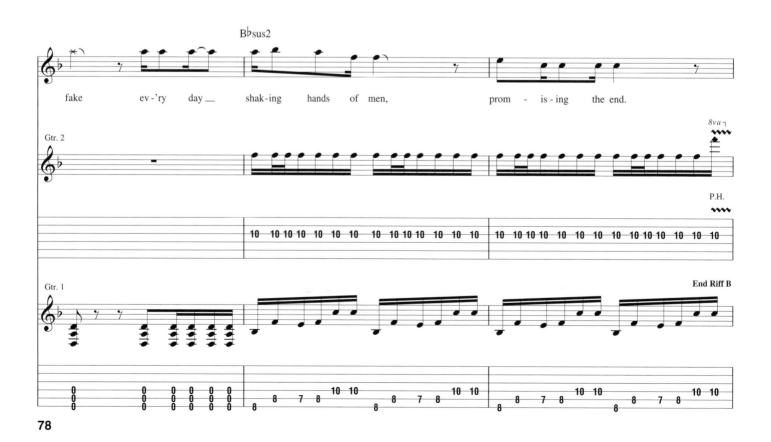

fake ev -'ry day ___ shak - ing hands of men, prom - is - ing the end.

Gtr. 2

P.H.

Gtr. 1

End Riff B

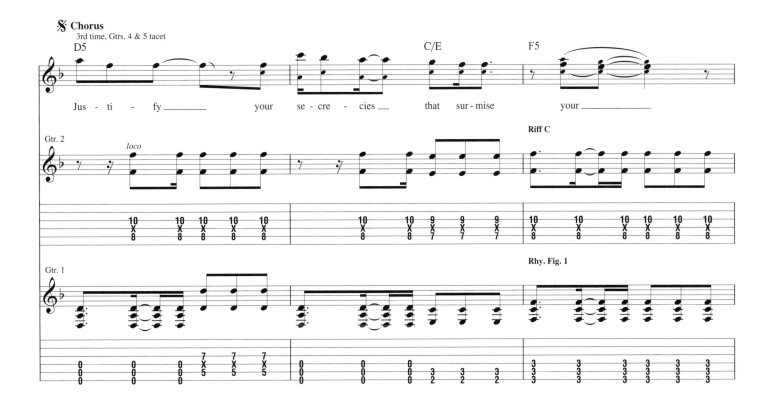

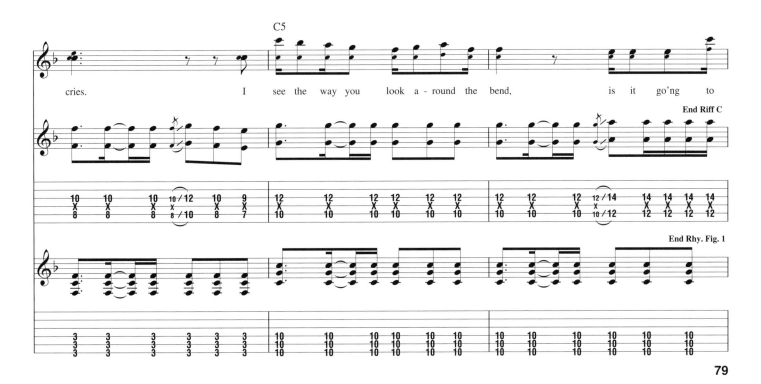

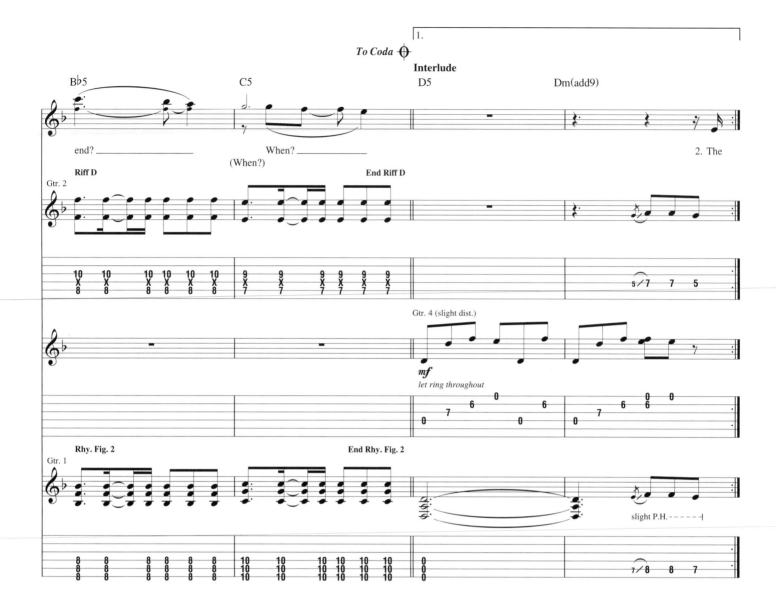

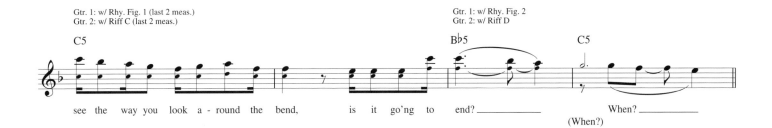

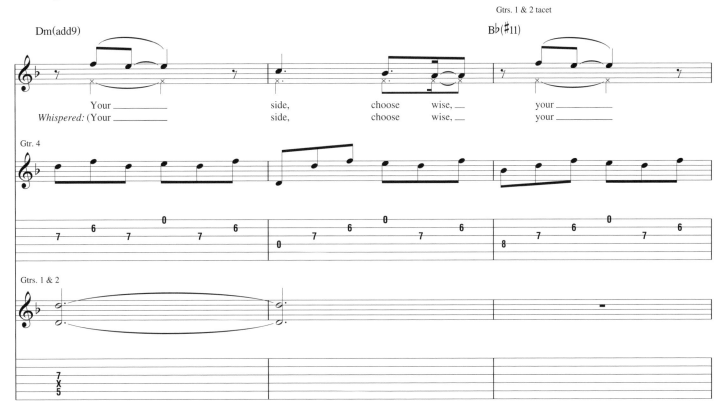

Bridge

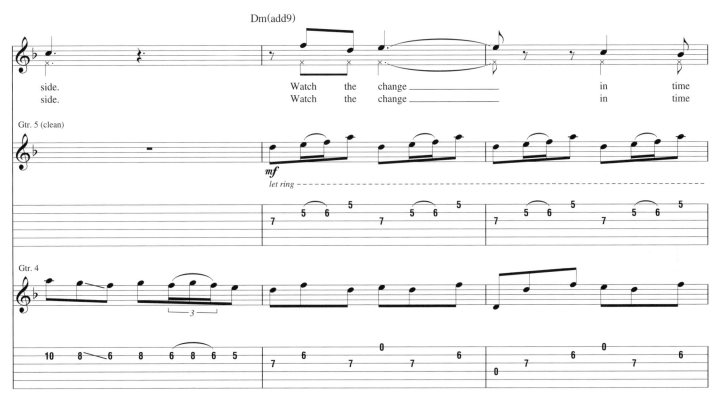

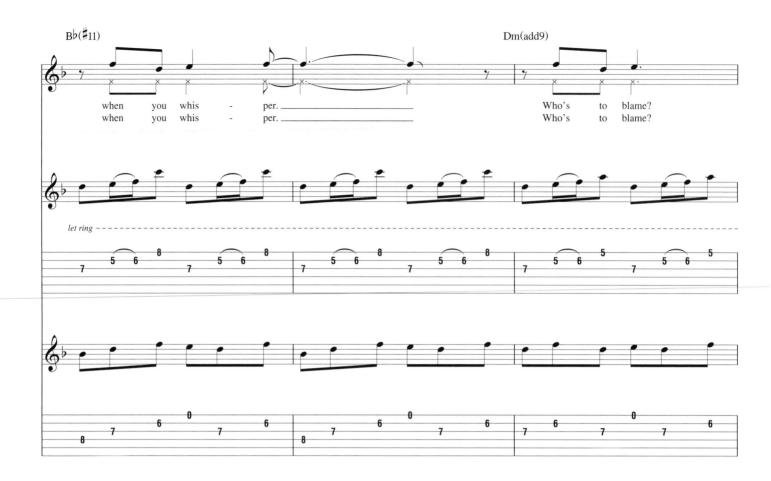

when you whis - per. _____ Who's to blame?
when you whis - per. _____ Who's to blame?

let ring -

D.S. al Coda

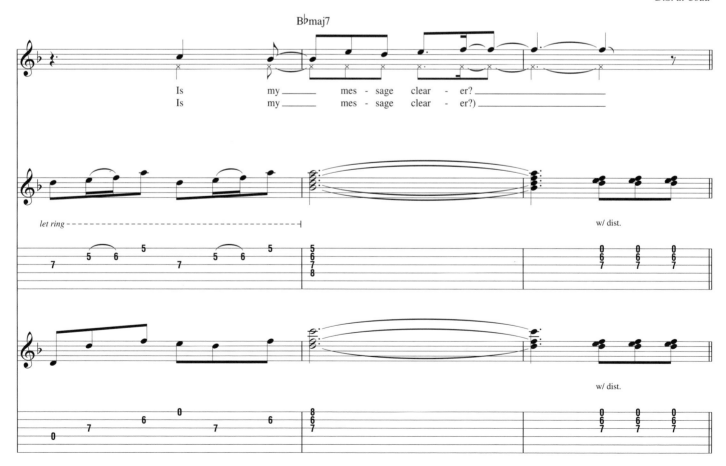

Is my _____ mes - sage clear - er? _____
Is my _____ mes - sage clear - er?) _____

let ring -

w/ dist.

w/ dist.

Your Guardian Angel

Words and Music by Ronnie Winter

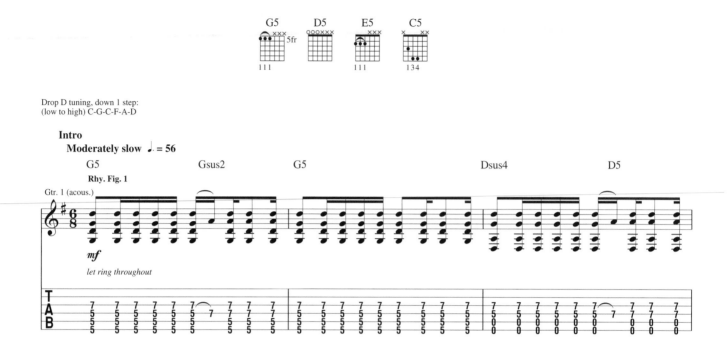

Drop D tuning, down 1 step:
(low to high) C-G-C-F-A-D

Intro
Moderately slow ♩ = 56

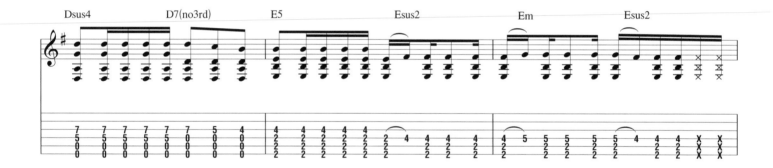

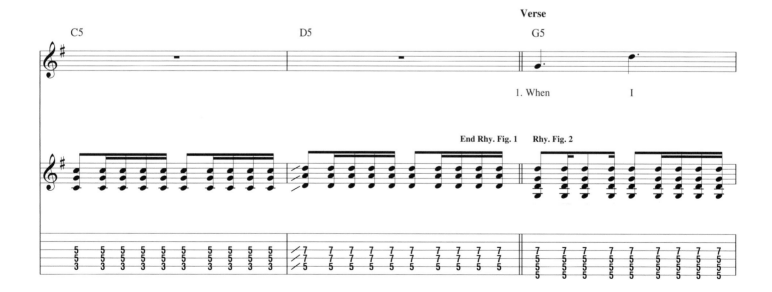

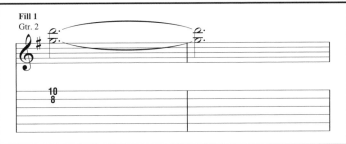

my true __ love, my whole __ heart. Please don't __ roll right a - way _____ 'cause

I'm here, here _____ for __ you. _____ Please __

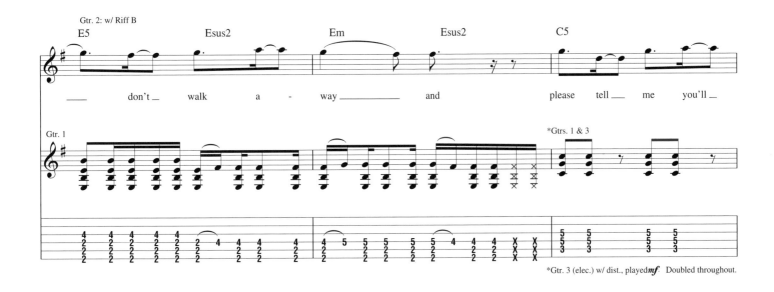

__ don't __ walk a - way _____ and please tell __ me you'll

*Gtr. 3 (elec.) w/ dist., played $\boldsymbol{mf}$. Doubled throughout.

Gtr. 1: w/ Rhy. Fig. 1 (1st 5 meas.)

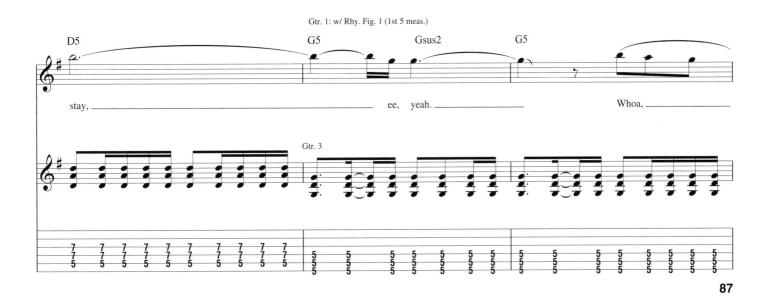

stay, _____ ee, yeah. _____ Whoa, _____

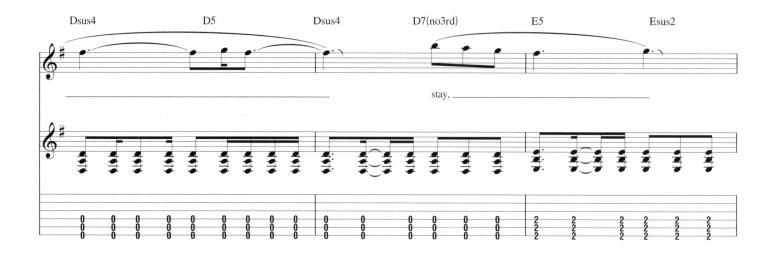

stay,

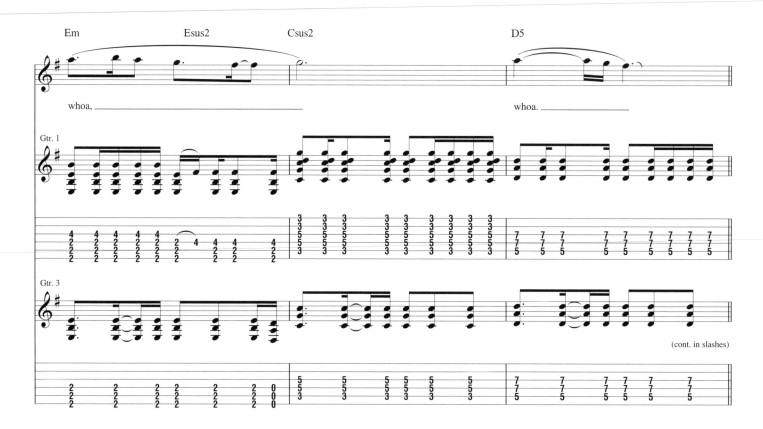

whoa,

whoa.

Gtr. 1

(cont. in slashes)

Gtr. 3

Outro-Chorus

Gtr. 1: w/ Rhy. Fig. 2 (till fade)

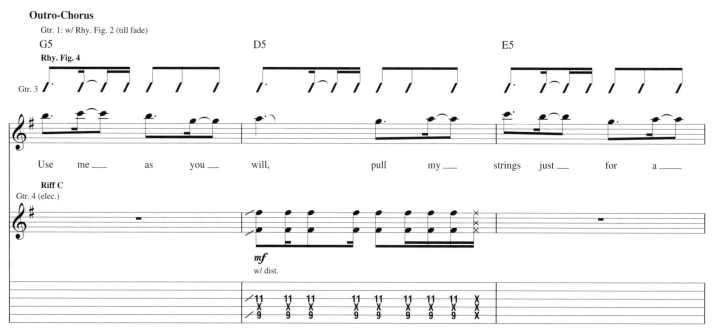

Use me ___ as you ___ will, pull my ___ strings just ___ for a ___

Riff C

Gtr. 4 (elec.)

mf

w/ dist.

88

thrill. _____ And I know I'll ___ be o - kay though my

skies are ___ tun - ing ___ gray.   I will nev - er ___ let you ___ fall,

Bkgd. Voc.: w/ Voc. Fig. 1 (till fade)

*w/ echo set for dotted quarter-note regeneration, w/ 2 repeats.

2nd time, Begin fade

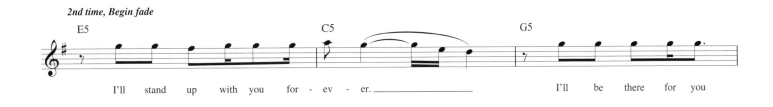

I'll stand up with you for - ev - er. _____ I'll be there for you

through it ___ all   e - ven if sav - ing you sends me ___ to heav - en.

Fade out

I will nev - er ___ let you ___ fall,   I'll stand up with you for...

89

Grim Goodbye

Words and Music by Ronnie Winter

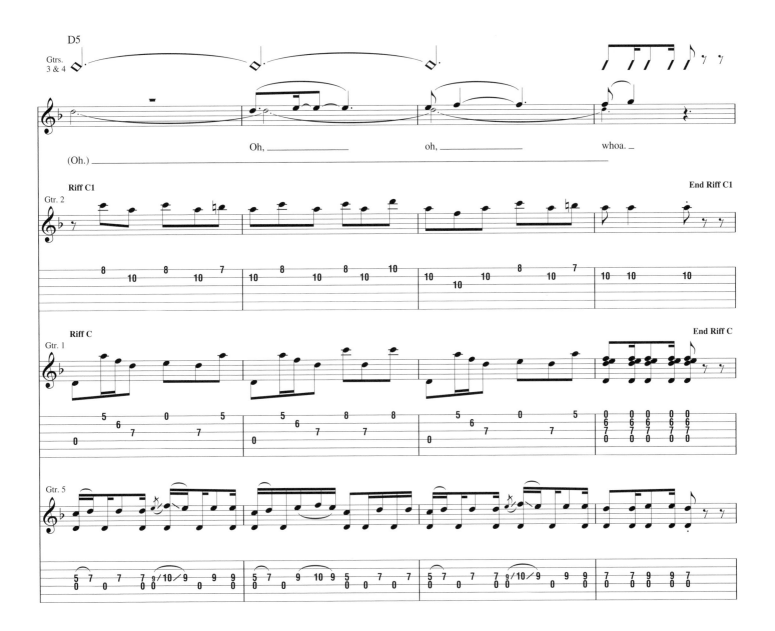

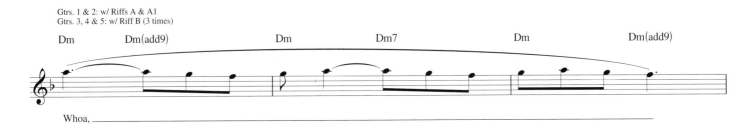

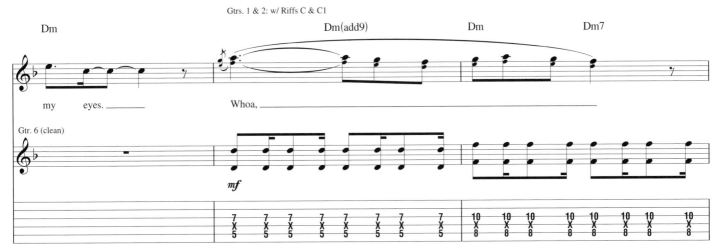

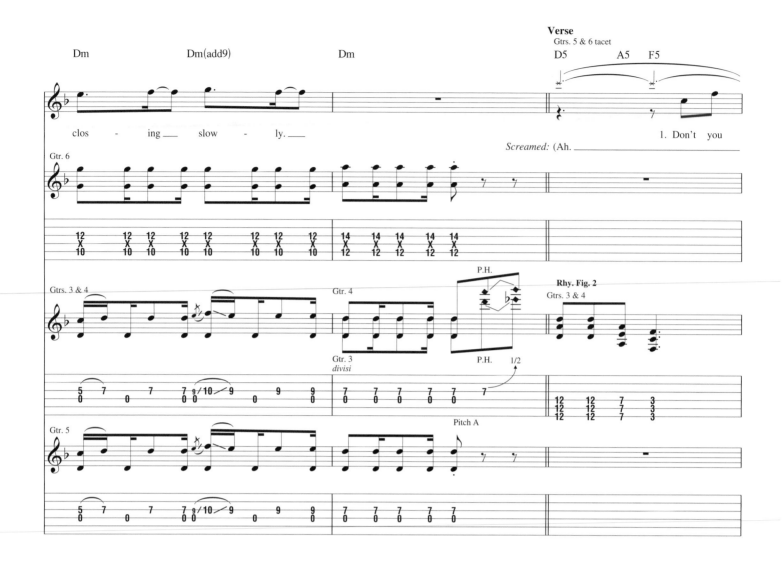

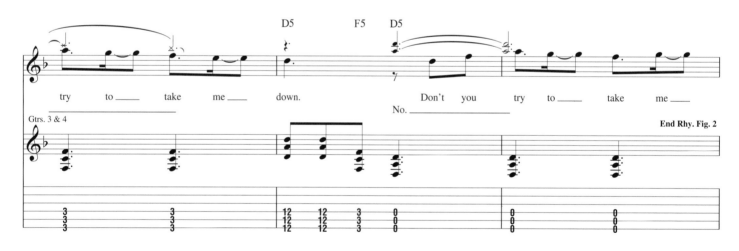

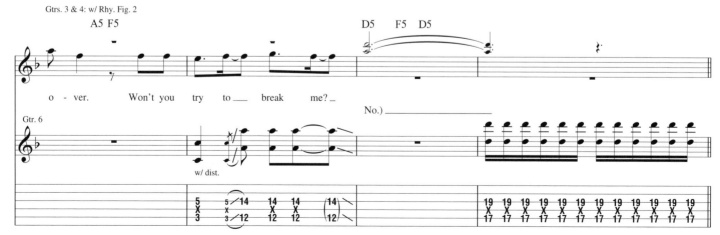

Verse

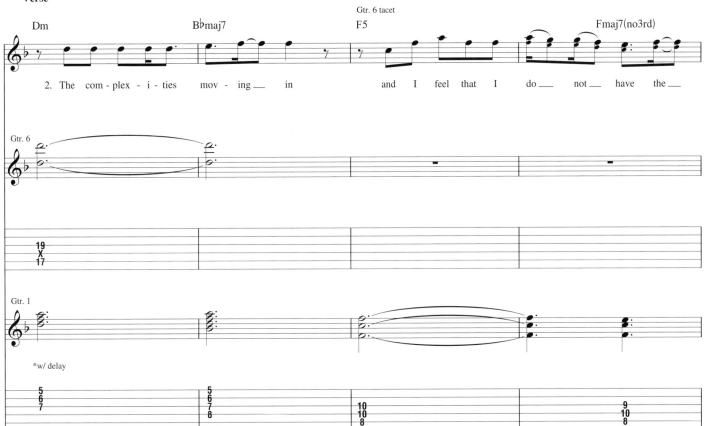

*w/ delay

*Set for quarter-note regeneration w/ 1 repeat.

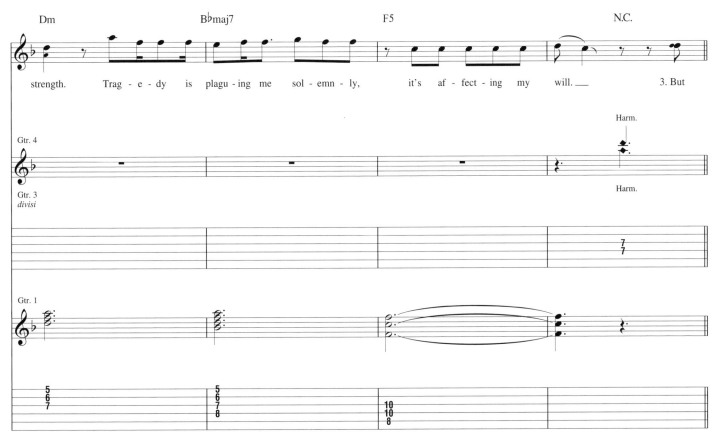

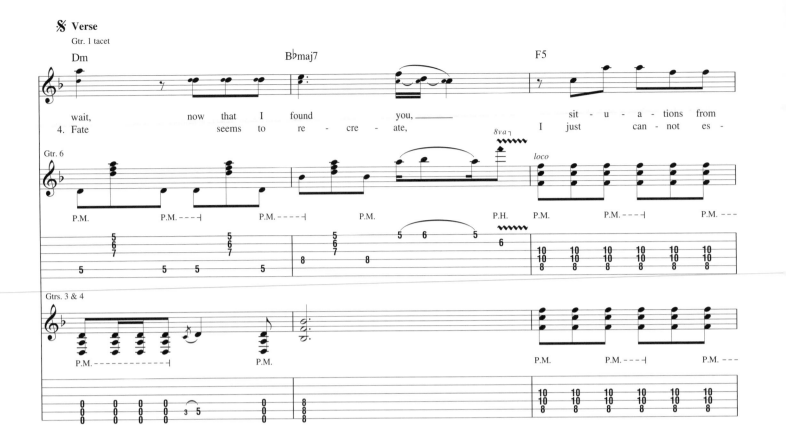

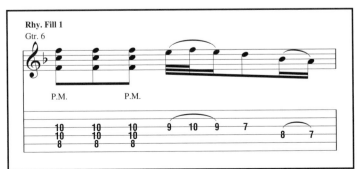

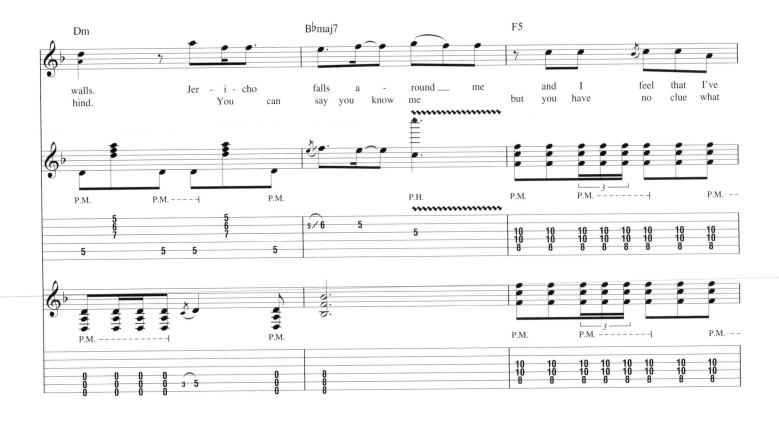

walls.   Jer - i - cho   falls a - round — me   and I   feel that I've

hind.   You can   say you know me   but you have   no clue what

Pre-Chorus

Gtrs. 3 & 6 tacet
2nd time, Gtr. 1: w/ Fill 1

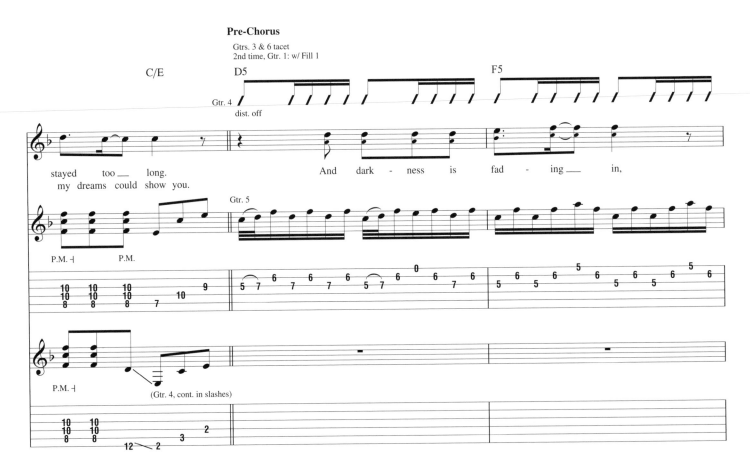

stayed too — long.

my dreams could show you.   And dark - ness is   fad - ing — in,

Fill 1

Gtr. 1

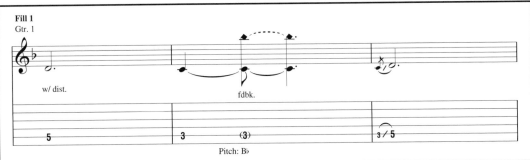

w/ dist.   fdbk.

Pitch: B♭

Coda 1

Interlude

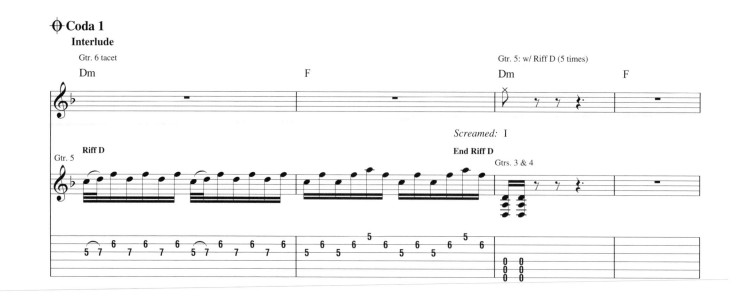

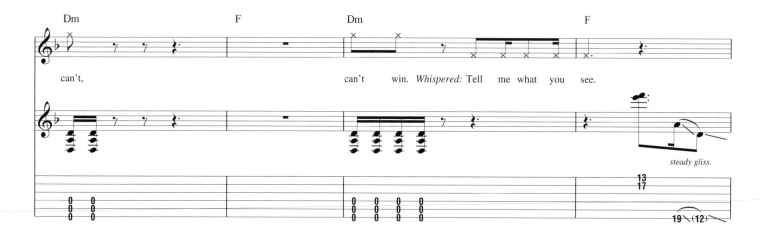

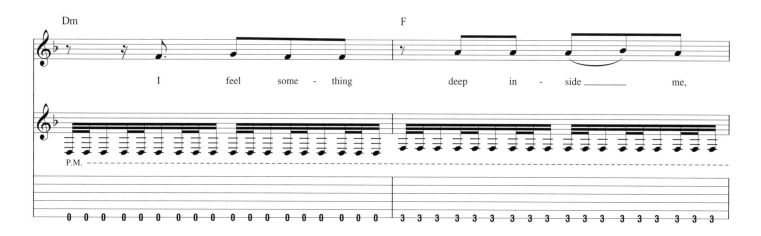

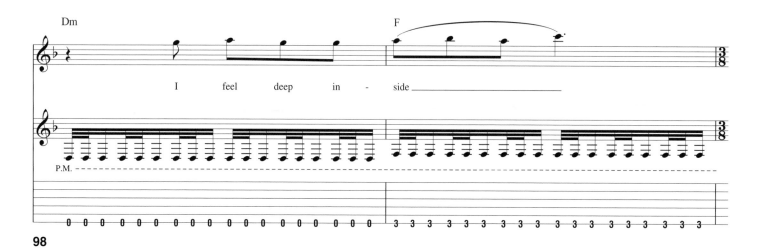

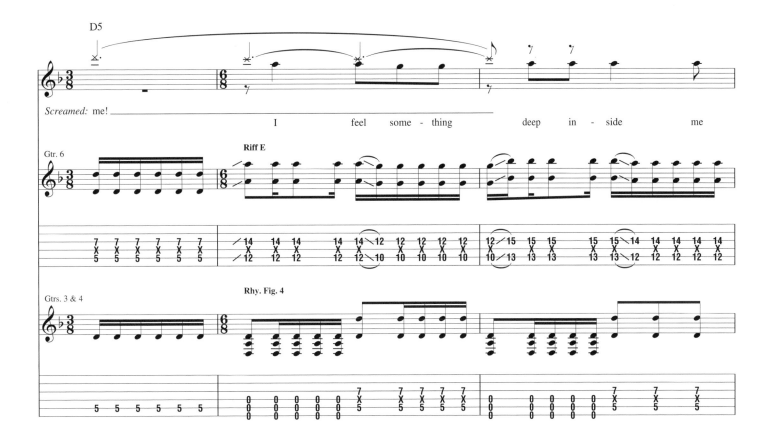

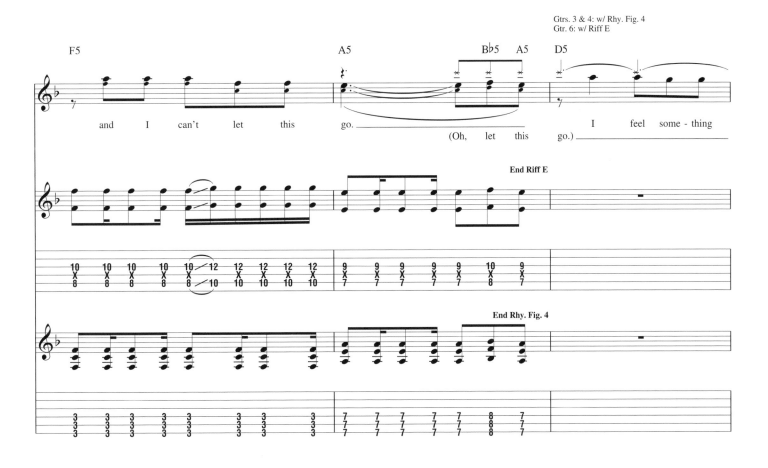

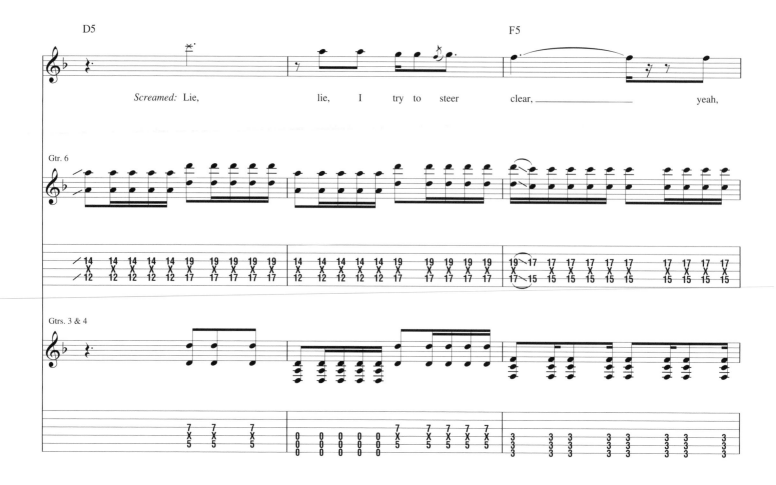

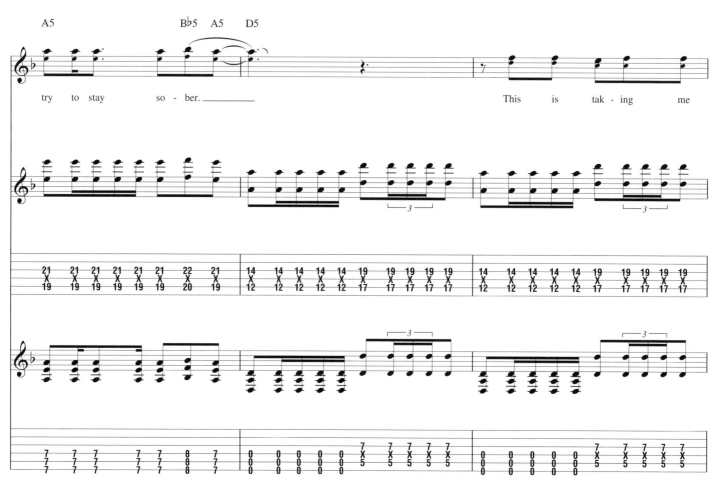

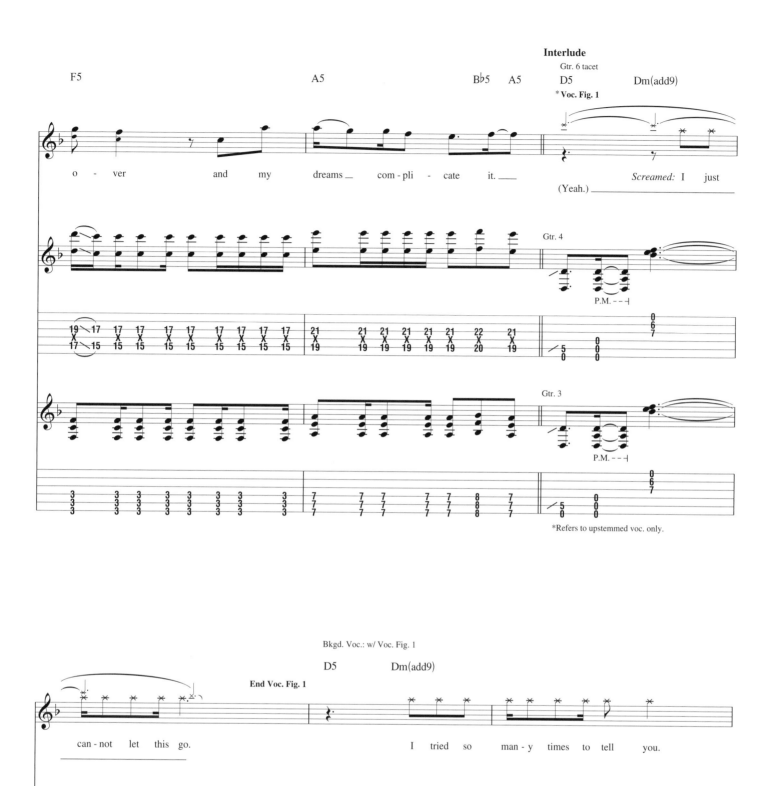

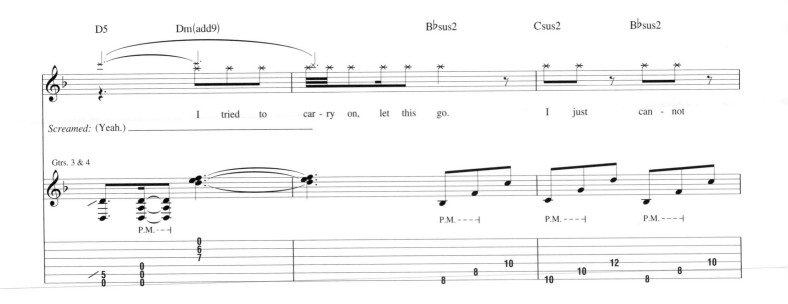

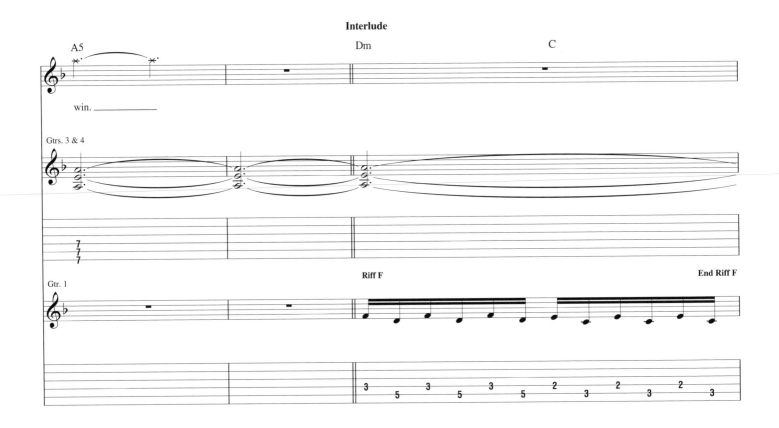

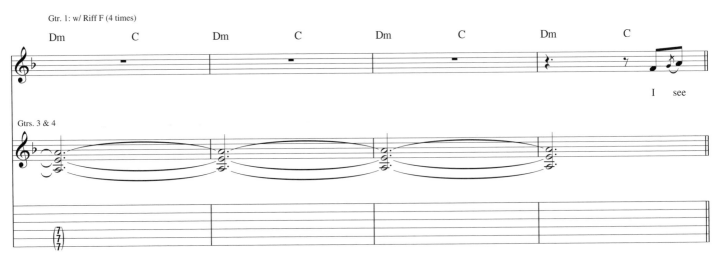

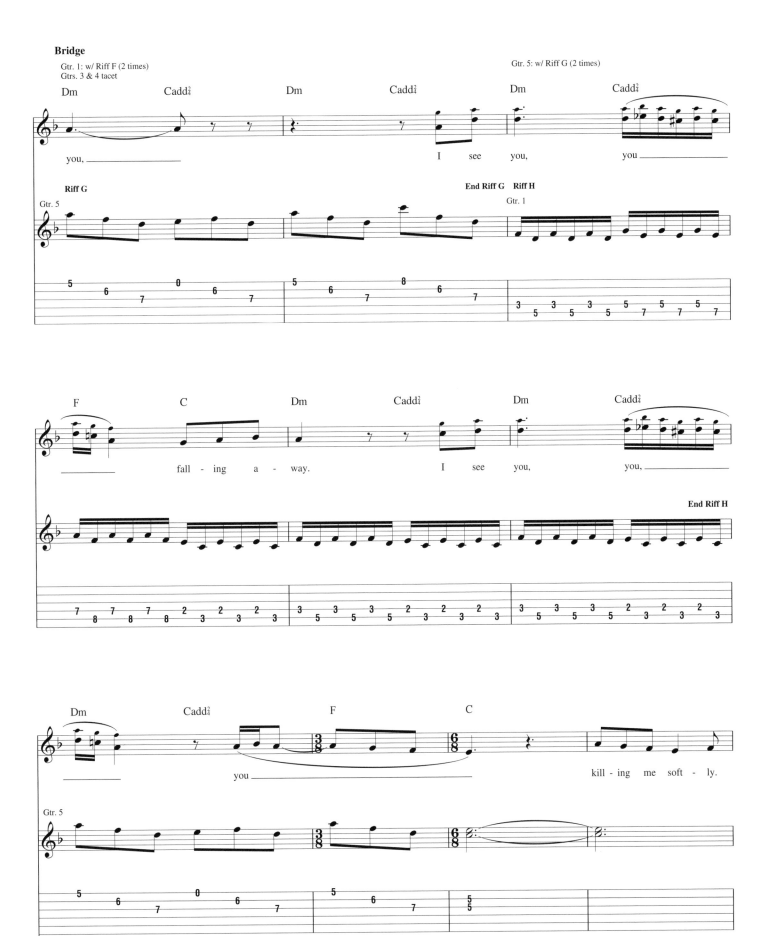

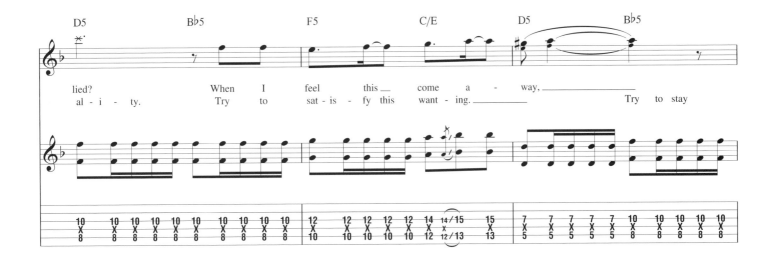

Interlude

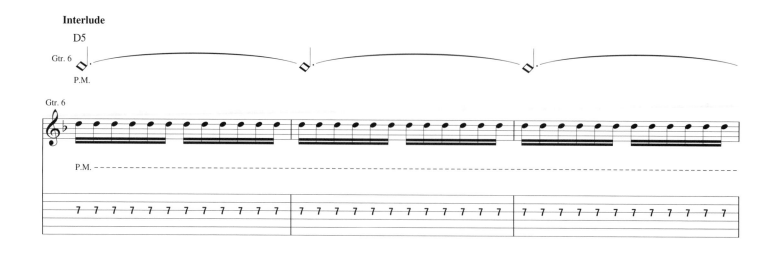

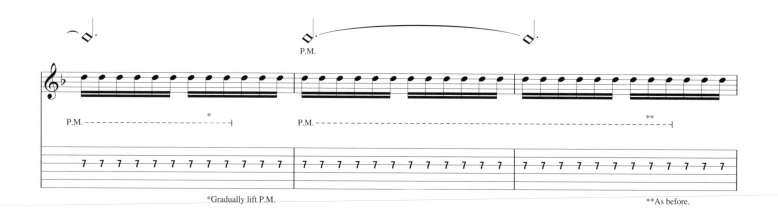

*Gradually lift P.M.   **As before.

Interlude

Gtr. 6 tacet

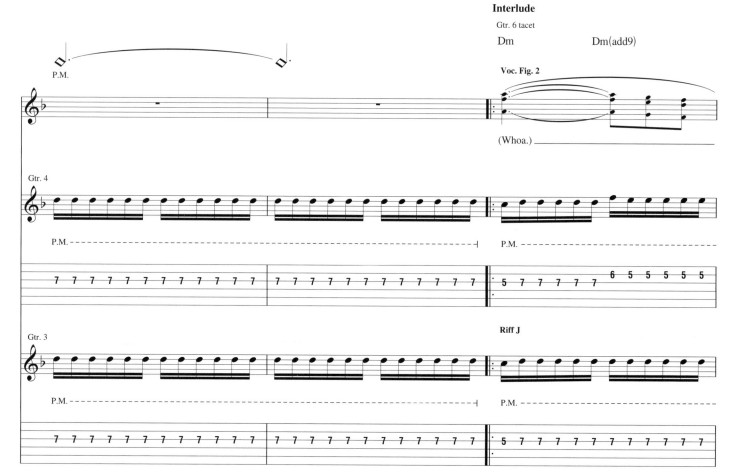

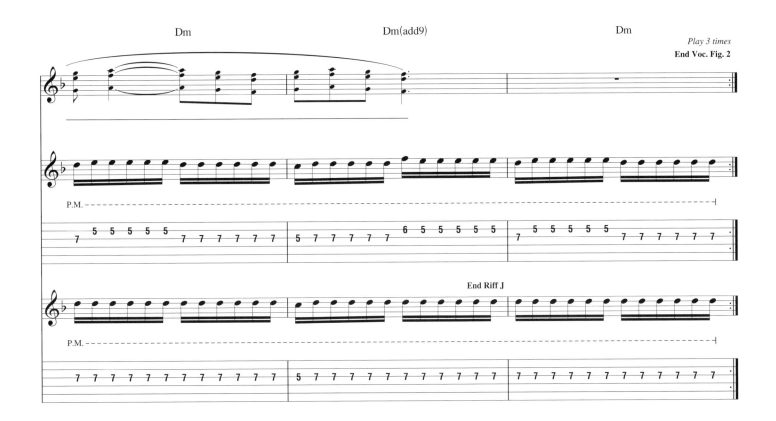

Bkgd. Voc.: w/ Voc. Fig. 2 (3 times)
Gtr. 3: w/ Riff J

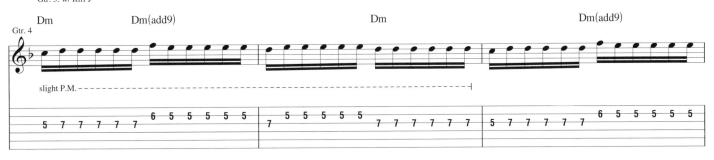

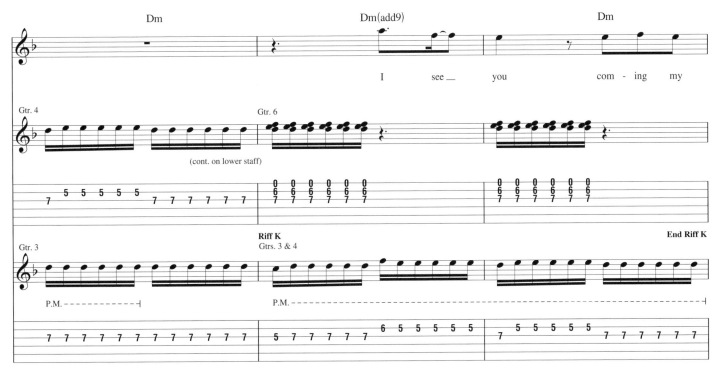

Gtrs. 3 & 4: w/ Riff K (1 1/2 times)

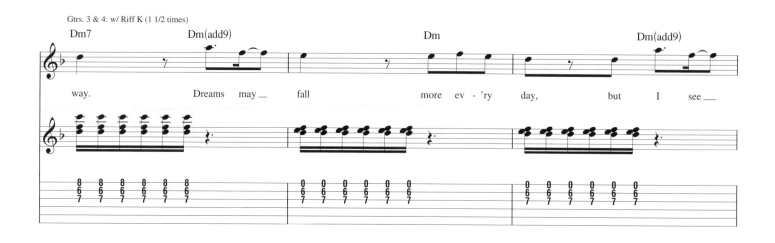

way. Dreams may __ fall more ev - 'ry day, but I see __

D.S.S. al Coda 2

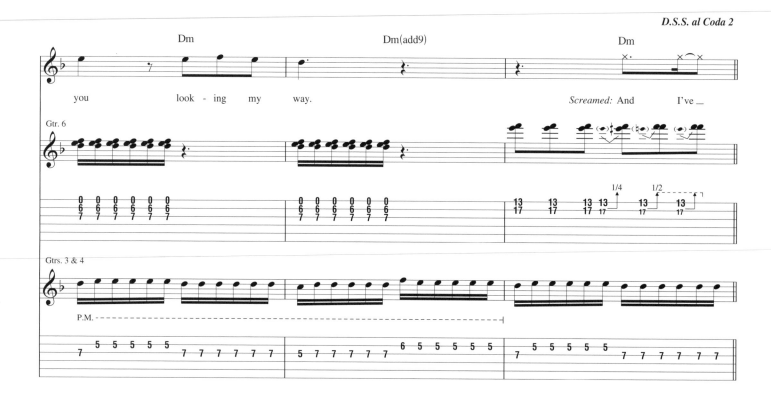

you look - ing my way. *Screamed:* And I've __

Gtr. 6

Gtrs. 3 & 4

P.M.

$\oplus$ **Coda 2**

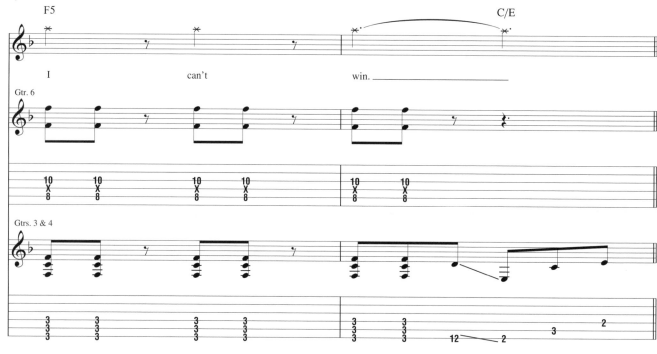

I can't win. __

Gtr. 6

Gtrs. 3 & 4

108

Outro

Gtrs. 3, 4 & 6 tacet
Gtr. 5: w/ Riff D (3 times)

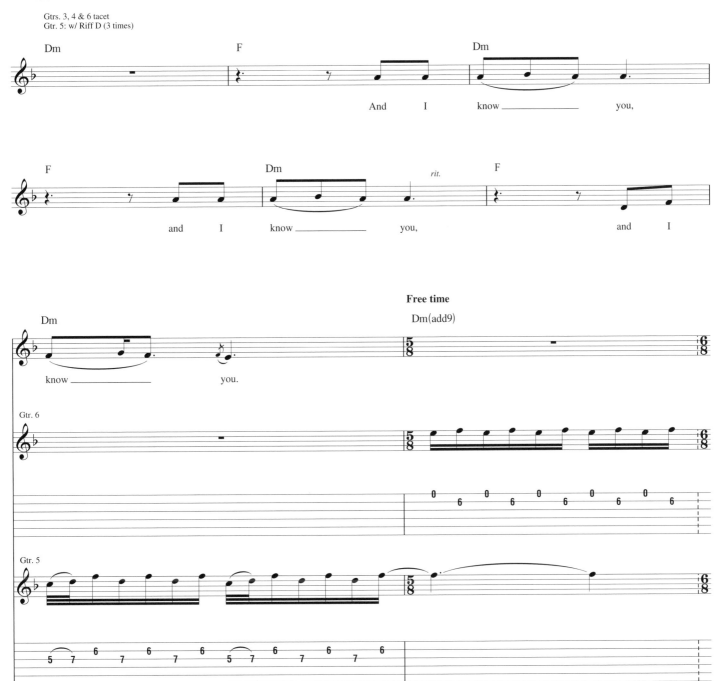

And I know _____ you,

and I know _____ you,

and I

rit.

Free time

Dm(add9)

know _____ you.

Gtr. 6

Gtr. 5

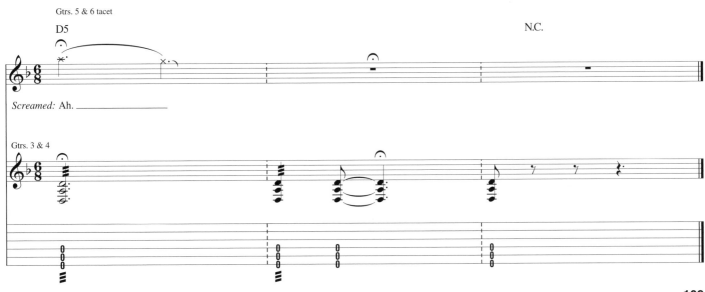

Gtrs. 5 & 6 tacet

D5

N.C.

Screamed: Ah. _____

Gtrs. 3 & 4

Guitar Notation Legend

Guitar music can be notated three different ways: on a *musical staff*, in *tablature*, and in *rhythm slashes*.

RHYTHM SLASHES are written above the staff. Strum chords in the rhythm indicated. Use the chord diagrams found at the top of the first page of the transcription for the appropriate chord voicings. Round noteheads indicate single notes.

THE MUSICAL STAFF shows pitches and rhythms and is divided by bar lines into measures. Pitches are named after the first seven letters of the alphabet.

TABLATURE graphically represents the guitar fingerboard. Each horizontal line represents a string, and each number represents a fret.

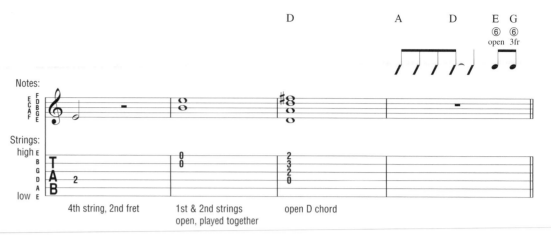

4th string, 2nd fret

1st & 2nd strings open, played together

open D chord

Definitions for Special Guitar Notation

HALF-STEP BEND: Strike the note and bend up 1/2 step.

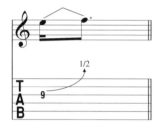

WHOLE-STEP BEND: Strike the note and bend up one step.

GRACE NOTE BEND: Strike the note and immediately bend up as indicated.

SLIGHT (MICROTONE) BEND: Strike the note and bend up 1/4 step.

BEND AND RELEASE: Strike the note and bend up as indicated, then release back to the original note. Only the first note is struck.

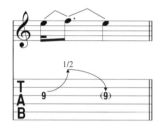

PRE-BEND: Bend the note as indicated, then strike it.

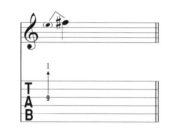

PRE-BEND AND RELEASE: Bend the note as indicated. Strike it and release the bend back to the original note.

UNISON BEND: Strike the two notes simultaneously and bend the lower note up to the pitch of the higher.

VIBRATO: The string is vibrated by rapidly bending and releasing the note with the fretting hand.

WIDE VIBRATO: The pitch is varied to a greater degree by vibrating with the fretting hand.

HAMMER-ON: Strike the first (lower) note with one finger, then sound the higher note (on the same string) with another finger by fretting it without picking.

PULL-OFF: Place both fingers on the notes to be sounded. Strike the first note and without picking, pull the finger off to sound the second (lower) note.

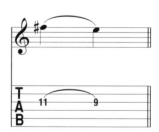

LEGATO SLIDE: Strike the first note and then slide the same fret-hand finger up or down to the second note. The second note is not struck.

SHIFT SLIDE: Same as legato slide, except the second note is struck.

TRILL: Very rapidly alternate between the notes indicated by continuously hammering on and pulling off.

TAPPING: Hammer ("tap") the fret indicated with the pick-hand index or middle finger and pull off to the note fretted by the fret hand.

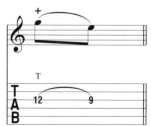

NATURAL HARMONIC: Strike the note while the fret-hand lightly touches the string directly over the fret indicated.

PINCH HARMONIC: The note is fretted normally and a harmonic is produced by adding the edge of the thumb or the tip of the index finger of the pick hand to the normal pick attack.

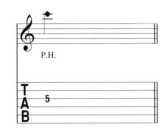

HARP HARMONIC: The note is fretted normally and a harmonic is produced by gently resting the pick hand's index finger directly above the indicated fret (in parentheses) while the pick hand's thumb or pick assists by plucking the appropriate string.

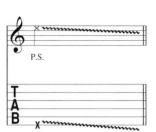

PICK SCRAPE: The edge of the pick is rubbed down (or up) the string, producing a scratchy sound.

MUFFLED STRINGS: A percussive sound is produced by laying the fret hand across the string(s) without depressing, and striking them with the pick hand.

PALM MUTING: The note is partially muted by the pick hand lightly touching the string(s) just before the bridge.

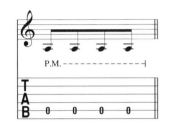

RAKE: Drag the pick across the strings indicated with a single motion.

TREMOLO PICKING: The note is picked as rapidly and continuously as possible.

ARPEGGIATE: Play the notes of the chord indicated by quickly rolling them from bottom to top.

VIBRATO BAR DIVE AND RETURN: The pitch of the note or chord is dropped a specified number of steps (in rhythm), then returned to the original pitch.

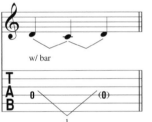

VIBRATO BAR SCOOP: Depress the bar just before striking the note, then quickly release the bar.

VIBRATO BAR DIP: Strike the note and then immediately drop a specified number of steps, then release back to the original pitch.

Additional Musical Definitions

 (accent)	• Accentuate note (play it louder).	

(accent)	• Accentuate note with great intensity.
(staccato)	• Play the note short.
⊓	• Downstroke
V	• Upstroke

D.S. al Coda
• Go back to the sign (𝄋), then play until the measure marked *"To Coda,"* then skip to the section labelled *"Coda."*

D.C. al Fine
• Go back to the beginning of the song and play until the measure marked *"Fine"* (end).

Rhy. Fig.
• Label used to recall a recurring accompaniment pattern (usually chordal).

Riff
• Label used to recall composed, melodic lines (usually single notes) which recur.

Fill
• Label used to identify a brief melodic figure which is to be inserted into the arrangement.

Rhy. Fill
• A chordal version of a Fill.

tacet
• Instrument is silent (drops out).

• Repeat measures between signs.

• When a repeated section has different endings, play the first ending only the first time and the second ending only the second time.

NOTE: Tablature numbers in parentheses mean:
1. The note is being sustained over a system (note in standard notation is tied), or
2. The note is sustained, but a new articulation (such as a hammer-on, pull-off, slide or vibrato) begins, or
3. The note is a barely audible "ghost" note (note in standard notation is also in parentheses).

RECORDED VERSIONS®
The Best Note-For-Note Transcriptions Available

ALL BOOKS INCLUDE TABLATURE

00692015	Aerosmith – Greatest Hits...........$22.95
00690603	Aerosmith – O Yeah! (Ultimate Hits) $24.95
00690178	Alice in Chains – Acoustic $19.95
00694865	Alice in Chains – Dirt....................$19.95
00690387	Alice in Chains – Nothing Safe: The Best of the Box $19.95
00690812	All American Rejects – Move Along $19.95
00694932	Allman Brothers Band – Volume 1 ....$24.95
00694933	Allman Brothers Band – Volume 2 ....$24.95
00694934	Allman Brothers Band – Volume 3 ....$24.95
00690865	Atreyu – A Deathgrip on Yesterday $19.95
00690609	Audioslave $19.95
00690804	Audioslave – Out of Exile $19.95
00690884	Audioslave – Revelations $19.95
00690820	Avenged Sevenfold – City of Evil $22.95
00690366	Bad Company – Original Anthology, Book 1 ....$19.95
00690503	Beach Boys – Very Best of $19.95
00690489	Beatles – 1 ....$24.95
00694929	Beatles – 1962-1966 ....$24.95
00694930	Beatles – 1967-1970 ....$24.95
00694832	Beatles – For Acoustic Guitar $22.95
00690110	Beatles – White Album (Book 1) $19.95
00692385	Chuck Berry $19.95
00690835	Billy Talent $19.95
00692200	Black Sabbath – We Sold Our Soul for Rock 'N' Roll $19.95
00690674	blink-182 ....$19.95
00690831	blink-182 – Greatest Hits $19.95
00690491	David Bowie – Best of $19.95
00690873	Breaking Benjamin – Phobia $19.95
00690764	Breaking Benjamin – We Are Not Alone $19.95
00690451	Jeff Buckley – Collection $24.95
00690590	Eric Clapton – Anthology................$29.95
00690415	Clapton Chronicles – Best of Eric Clapton ..$18.95
00690074	Eric Clapton – The Cream of Clapton $24.95
00690716	Eric Clapton – Me and Mr. Johnson $19.95
00694869	Eric Clapton – Unplugged $22.95
00690162	The Clash – Best of $19.95
00690828	Coheed & Cambria – Good Apollo I'm Burning Star, IV, Vol. 1: From Fear Through the Eyes of Madness $19.95
00690593	Coldplay – A Rush of Blood to the Head.....$19.95
00690838	Cream – Royal Albert Hall: London May 2-3-5-6 2005 ....$22.95
00690856	Creed – Greatest Hits $22.95
00690401	Creed – Human Clay $19.95
00690819	Creedence Clearwater Revival – Best of......$19.95
00690572	Steve Cropper – Soul Man $19.95
00690613	Crosby, Stills & Nash – Best of $19.95
00690289	Deep Purple – Best of $17.95
00690784	Def Leppard – Best of $19.95
00690347	The Doors – Anthology $22.95
00690348	The Doors – Essential Guitar Collection $16.95
00690810	Fall Out Boy – From Under the Cork Tree ..$19.95
00690664	Fleetwood Mac – Best of $19.95
00690870	Flyleaf $19.95
00690808	Foo Fighters – In Your Honor $19.95
00690805	Robben Ford – Best of $19.95
00694920	Free – Best of......................$19.95
00690848	Godsmack – IV $19.95
00690601	Good Charlotte – The Young and the Hopeless $19.95
00690697	Jim Hall – Best of $19.95
00690840	Ben Harper – Both Sides of the Gun $19.95
00694798	George Harrison – Anthology................$19.95
00692930	Jimi Hendrix – Are You Experienced?.........$24.95

00692931	Jimi Hendrix – Axis: Bold As Love $22.95
00690608	Jimi Hendrix – Blue Wild Angel $24.95
00692932	Jimi Hendrix – Electric Ladyland $24.95
00690017	Jimi Hendrix – Live at Woodstock $24.95
00690602	Jimi Hendrix – Smash Hits $19.95
00690843	H.I.M. – Dark Light $19.95
00690869	Hinder – Extreme Behavior $19.95
00690692	Billy Idol – Very Best of $19.95
00690688	Incubus – A Crow Left of the Murder $19.95
00690457	Incubus – Make Yourself $19.95
00690544	Incubus – Morningview $19.95
00690790	Iron Maiden Anthology $24.95
00690730	Alan Jackson – Guitar Collection $19.95
00690721	Jet – Get Born $19.95
00690684	Jethro Tull – Aqualung $19.95
00690647	Jewel – Best of $19.95
00690814	John5 – Songs for Sanity $19.95
00690751	John5 – Vertigo $19.95
00690845	Eric Johnson – Bloom $19.95
00690846	Jack Johnson and Friends – Sing-A-Longs and Lullabies for the Film Curious George $19.95
00690271	Robert Johnson – New Transcriptions.....$24.95
00699131	Janis Joplin – Best of $19.95
00690427	Judas Priest – Best of $19.95
00690742	The Killers – Hot Fuss $19.95
00694903	Kiss – Best of $24.95
00690780	Korn – Greatest Hits, Volume 1 ....$22.95
00690834	Lamb of God – Ashes of the Wake $19.95
00690875	Lamb of God – Sacrament $19.95
00690823	Ray LaMontagne – Trouble $19.95
00690679	John Lennon – Guitar Collection $19.95
00690781	Linkin Park – Hybrid Theory $22.95
00690782	Linkin Park – Meteora $22.95
00690783	Live – Best of $19.95
00690743	Los Lonely Boys $19.95
00690876	Los Lonely Boys – Sacred $19.95
00690720	Lostprophets – Start Something.............$19.95
00694954	Lynyrd Skynyrd – New Best of.............$19.95
00690752	Lynyrd Skynyrd – Street Survivors.........$19.95
00690577	Yngwie Malmsteen – Anthology............$24.95
00690754	Marilyn Manson – Lest We Forget $19.95
00694956	Bob Marley– Legend $19.95
00694945	Bob Marley– Songs of Freedom $24.95
00690657	Maroon5 – Songs About Jane................$19.95
00120080	Don McLean – Songbook $19.95
00694951	Megadeth – Rust in Peace $22.95
00690768	Megadeth – The System Has Failed $19.95
00690505	John Mellencamp – Guitar Collection $19.95
00690646	Pat Metheny – One Quiet Night............$19.95
00690558	Pat Metheny – Trio: 99>00 ....$19.95
00690040	Steve Miller Band – Young Hearts $19.95
00690794	Mudvayne – Lost and Found.............$19.95
00690611	Nirvana $22.95
00694883	Nirvana – Nevermind $19.95
00690026	Nirvana – Unplugged in New York $19.95
00690807	The Offspring – Greatest Hits $19.95
00694847	Ozzy Osbourne – Best of $22.95
00690399	Ozzy Osbourne – Ozzman Cometh.........$19.95
00690866	Panic! At the Disco – A Fever You Can't Sweat Out $19.95
00694855	Pearl Jam – Ten $19.95
00690439	A Perfect Circle – Mer De Noms.........$19.95
00690661	A Perfect Circle – Thirteenth Step $19.95
00690499	Tom Petty – Definitive Guitar Collection $19.95
00690428	Pink Floyd – Dark Side of the Moon $19.95
00690789	Poison – Best of...................$19.95
00693864	The Police – Best of $19.95

00694975	Queen – Greatest Hits $24.95
00690670	Queensryche – Very Best of.............$19.95
00690878	The Raconteurs – Broken Boy Soldiers $19.95
00694910	Rage Against the Machine $19.95
00690055	Red Hot Chili Peppers – Blood Sugar Sex Magik $19.95
00690584	Red Hot Chili Peppers – By the Way $19.95
00690379	Red Hot Chili Peppers – Californication $19.95
00690673	Red Hot Chili Peppers – Greatest Hits $19.95
00690852	Red Hot Chili Peppers – Stadium Arcadium $24.95
00690511	Django Reinhardt – Definitive Collection...$19.95
00690779	Relient K – MMHMM..................$19.95
00690643	Relient K – Two Lefts Don't Make a Right...But Three Do $19.95
00690631	Rolling Stones – Guitar Anthology $24.95
00690685	David Lee Roth – Eat 'Em and Smile.........$19.95
00690694	David Lee Roth – Guitar Anthology $24.95
00690031	Santana's Greatest Hits $19.95
00690796	Michael Schenker – Very Best of $19.95
00690566	Scorpions – Best of $19.95
00690604	Bob Seger – Guitar Collection $19.95
00690803	Kenny Wayne Shepherd Band – Best of $19.95
00690857	Shinedown – Us and Them $19.95
00690530	Slipknot – Iowa...................$19.95
00690733	Slipknot – Vol. 3 (The Subliminal Verses) ..$19.95
00120004	Steely Dan – Best of $24.95
00694921	Steppenwolf – Best of.................$22.95
00690655	Mike Stern – Best of.................$19.95
00690877	Stone Sour – Come What(ever) May $19.95
00690520	Styx Guitar Collection $19.95
00120081	Sublime...................$19.95
00690771	SUM 41 – Chuck $19.95
00690767	Switchfoot – The Beautiful Letdown $19.95
00690830	System of a Down – Hypnotize $19.95
00690799	System of a Down – Mezmerize...........$19.95
00690531	System of a Down – Toxicity...........$19.95
00694824	James Taylor – Best of $16.95
00690871	Three Days Grace – One-X $19.95
00690737	3 Doors Down – The Better Life...............$22.95
00690683	Robin Trower – Bridge of Sighs $19.95
00690740	Shania Twain – Guitar Collection $19.95
00699191	U2 – Best of: 1980-1990................$19.95
00690732	U2 – Best of: 1990-2000................$19.95
00690775	U2 – How to Dismantle an Atomic Bomb ...$22.95
00690575	Steve Vai – Alive in an Ultra World $22.95
00660137	Steve Vai – Passion & Warfare $24.95
00690116	Stevie Ray Vaughan – Guitar Collection.......$24.95
00660058	Stevie Ray Vaughan – Lightnin' Blues 1983-1987...........$24.95
00694835	Stevie Ray Vaughan – The Sky Is Crying $22.95
00690015	Stevie Ray Vaughan – Texas Flood $19.95
00690772	Velvet Revolver – Contraband..................$22.95
00690071	Weezer (The Blue Album) $19.95
00690447	The Who – Best of...................$24.95
00690589	ZZ Top Guitar Anthology................$22.95